Service in the Trenches

Service in the Trenches

School Principals Share True Stories of Servant Leadership

Edited by

Rocky Wallace

with

Eve Proffitt and Stephanie Sullivan

ROWMAN & LITTLEFIELD
Lanham • Boulder • New York • London

Published by Rowman & Littlefield
An imprint of The Rowman & Littlefield Publishing Group, Inc.
4501 Forbes Boulevard, Suite 200, Lanham, Maryland 20706
www.rowman.com
86-90 Paul Street, London EC2A 4NE, United Kingdom

Copyright © 2023 by Rocky Wallace

All rights reserved. No part of this book may be reproduced in any form or by any electronic or mechanical means, including information storage and retrieval systems, without written permission from the publisher, except by a reviewer who may quote passages in a review.

British Library Cataloguing in Publication Information Available

Library of Congress Cataloging-in-Publication Data Available

ISBN 978-1-4758-6699-5 (cloth) | ISBN 978-1-4758-6700-8 (pbk.)
   978-1-4758-6701-5 (ebook)

A project like this cannot be completed without the sacrifice of time and talents of all who contribute in so many ways. So, to Dr. Tom Koerner and his team at Rowman & Littlefield, the chapter authors who shared such powerful true stories, endorsement contributors, co-editors Dr. Stephanie Sullivan and Dr. Eve Proffitt, and to the educational leaders in the trenches who tirelessly work every day to grow great schools, we dedicate this book . . .

Special credit to the Kentucky Department of Education and its coordinating of our University Principal Preparation Initiative, as the continued support and facilitation of this collaborative team is a blessing to all of us involved and is the catalyst for this, our second book on school improvement.

Contents

Foreword *Larry C. Spears*	ix
Introduction *Lu Young*	xv
1: The Rookie *Rocky Wallace*	1
2: The Substitute *Mike Hylen*	7
3: Sacrifices *Carol Christian*	13
4: From Darkness to Light *Josh Gupton*	17
5: Pipeline *Jason Detre*	25
6: An Unlikely Administrator *Whitney Shannon Wilson*	29
7: Beth's Road to Servant Leadership *Rosemarie Young*	37
8: What Do You Need from Me?: (Especially Considering I Am Only Here Approximately Half of the Time?) *Lewis Willian*	43
9: COVID-19 *Tabetha Housekeeper*	47

10: Going and Driving the Extra Mile *Stephanie Sullivan*	55
11: Gideon's Story *J.P. Rader*	61
12: "Feed" Your People *Kelly Odell*	67
13: Changing the School's Positivity Image *William Sims*	73
14: Developing a Team *Myram Brady*	79
15: When It Rains, It Pours *Laura Beth Hayes*	85
16: 30 Minutes *Michael W. Kessinger*	91
17: What Servant Leadership Is and Is Not *Franklin Thomas*	99
18: Service: The Secret Ingredient to Successful Leadership *Carrie Ballinger*	105
19: The Milkman *Ann Burns*	111
Closing Thoughts: 9/11/2001 *Jay Cloud*	115
Afterword *Byron Darnall*	121
References	123
About the Editor and Contributors	127

Foreword

Larry C. Spears

I am honored to have been asked to write the Foreword to *Service in the Trenches: School Principals Share True Stories of Servant Leadership*. I would like to tell you briefly about servant leadership.

A life-long example of how things get done in organizations, Robert Greenleaf, who coined the term *servant leader* in his 1970 essay, "The Servant as Leader," was especially concerned with encouraging the understanding and practice of servant leadership within educational systems. In *The Power of Servant-Leadership* (Berrett-Koehler, 1998), *Servant Leadership, 25th Anniversary Edition*, (Paulist Press, 2002), *The Servant-Leader Within* (Paulist Press, 2003), and other books and essays, Greenleaf examined the process of teaching/learning and offered his thinking on how servant leadership could enhance the experiences of both students, teachers, and institutional leaders alike.

Who *is* a servant leader? Greenleaf said that the servant leader is one who is a servant first. In *The Servant as Leader* he wrote the following:

> It begins with the natural feeling that one wants to serve, to serve first. Then conscious choice brings one to aspire to lead. The difference manifests itself in the care taken by the servant—first to make sure that other people's highest priority needs are being served. The best test is: Do those served grow as persons; do they, while being served, become healthier, wiser, freer, more autonomous, more likely themselves to become servants? And, what is the effect on the least privileged in society? Will they benefit or at least not be further deprived?

It is important to remember that servant leadership begins within each of us. As a life-long student of how things get done in organizations, Greenleaf distilled his observations in a series of essays and books on the theme of "The

Servant as Leader"—the objective of which was to stimulate thought and action for building a better, more caring society.

The servant leader concept continues to grow in its influence and impact. In fact, we have witnessed a remarkable growth of awareness and practices of servant leadership. In many ways, it may be said that the times are only now beginning to catch up with Robert Greenleaf's visionary call to servant leadership. The idea of servant leadership, now in its sixth decade as a concept bearing that name, continues to create a quiet revolution around the world.

The words servant and leader are usually thought of as being opposites. In deliberately bringing those two words together in a meaningful way, Robert Greenleaf gave birth to the paradoxical term *servant leader*. Since 1970, many of today's most creative thinkers are writing and speaking about servant leadership as an emerging paradigm for the twenty-first century.

Robert Greenleaf's writings on the subject of servant leadership helped to get this movement started, and his views have had a profound and growing effect on many organizations and thought leaders. Organizations like Starbucks, TD Industries, The Toro Company, Southwest Airlines, Men's Wearhouse, Pieper Electric, Synovus Financial Corporation, The Container Store, Popeyes Restaurants, and many more are recognized today for nurturing servant-led cultures.

These and many more organizational practitioners have been encouraged and supported by a long list of thought leaders such as James Autry, Warren Bennis, Ken Blanchard, Peter Block, John Carver, Stephen Covey, Max DePree, Shann Ferch, Don Frick, John Horsman, Joseph Jaworski, James Kouzes, Larraine Matusak, Parker Palmer, Kathleen Patterson, M. Scott Peck, Peter Senge, Peter Vaill, Rocky Wallace, Margaret Wheatley, and Danah Zohar, to name just some of today's cutting-edge authors and advocates of servant leadership.

Some organizational leaders have concluded that servant leadership is the right thing to do and have subsequently embraced it. This has certainly been important as servant leadership has grown and advanced over the years. However, it is vitally important to note that Greenleaf titled his essay, "The Servant as Leader" and not "The Leader as Servant." While encouraging leaders to act as servants was and is a remarkable idea; asking servants to act as leaders was (and remains) a truly wonderful and radical idea. It is also an idea that goes against our limited expectations of contemporary culture. It is this fact that makes servant leadership such a unique and potent philosophy.

Robert K. Greenleaf is someone who thought and wrote a great deal about the nature of servant leadership and character. In 1992, when conducting a study of Robert Greenleaf's writings, the analysis codified a set of ten characteristics about which Greenleaf wrote and considered central to the development of servant leaders. These include the following.

- *Listening*: Leaders have traditionally been valued for their communication and decision-making skills. Although these are also important skills for the servant leader, they need to be reinforced by a deep commitment to listening intently to others. The servant leader seeks to identify the will of a group and helps to clarify that will. He or she listens receptively to what is being said and unsaid. Listening also encompasses hearing one's own inner voice. Listening, coupled with periods of reflection, is essential to the growth and well-being of the servant leader. For Robert Greenleaf, listening was the single most important characteristic of the effective servant leader.
- *Empathy*: The servant leader strives to understand and empathize with others. People need to be accepted and recognized for their special and unique spirits. One assumes the good intentions of co-workers and colleagues and does not reject them as people, even when one may be forced to refuse to accept certain behaviors or performance. The most successful servant leaders are those who have become skilled empathetic listeners.
- *Healing*: The healing of relationships is a powerful force for transformation and integration. One of the great strengths of servant leadership is the potential for healing one's self and one's relationship to others. Many people have broken spirits and have suffered from a variety of emotional hurts. Although this is a part of being human, servant leaders recognize that they have an opportunity to help make whole those with whom they come in contact. In his essay, "The Servant as Leader," Greenleaf writes, "There is something subtle communicated to one who is being served and led if, implicit in the compact between servant-leader and led, is the understanding that the search for wholeness is something they share."
- *Awareness*: General awareness, and especially self-awareness, strengthens the servant leader. Awareness helps one in understanding issues involving ethics, power, and values. It lends itself to being able to view most situations from a more integrated, holistic position. As Greenleaf observed: "Awareness is not a giver of solace—it is just the opposite. It is a disturber and an awakener. Able leaders are usually sharply awake and reasonably disturbed. They are not seekers after solace. They have their own inner serenity."
- *Persuasion*: Another characteristic of servant leaders is reliance on persuasion, rather than on one's positional authority, in making decisions within an organization. The servant leader seeks to convince others, rather than coerce compliance. This particular element offers one of the clearest distinctions between the traditional authoritarian model and that of servant leadership. The servant leader is effective at building

consensus within groups. This emphasis on persuasion over coercion finds its roots in the beliefs of the Religious Society of Friends (Quakers), the denominational body to which Robert Greenleaf belonged.

- *Conceptualization*: Servant leaders seek to nurture their abilities to dream great dreams. The ability to look at a problem or an organization from a conceptualizing perspective means that one must think beyond day-to-day realities. For many leaders, this is a characteristic that requires discipline and practice. The traditional leader is consumed by the need to achieve short-term operational goals. The leader who wishes to also be a servant leader must stretch his or her thinking to encompass broader-based conceptual thinking. Within organizations, conceptualization is, by its very nature, a key role of boards of trustees or directors. Trustees need to be mostly conceptual in their orientation, staffs need to be mostly operational in their perspective, and the most effective executive leaders probably need to develop both perspectives within themselves. Servant leaders are called to seek a delicate balance between conceptual thinking and a day-to-day operational approach.
- *Foresight*: Closely related to conceptualization, the ability to foresee the likely outcome of a situation is hard to define, but easier to identify. One knows foresight when one experiences it. Foresight is a characteristic that enables the servant leader to understand the lessons from the past, the realities of the present, and the likely consequence of a decision for the future. It is also deeply rooted within the intuitive mind. Foresight remains a largely unexplored area in leadership studies but one most deserving of careful attention.
- *Stewardship*: Peter Block, author of *Stewardship and The Empowered Manager*, has defined stewardship as "holding something in trust for another." Robert Greenleaf's view of all institutions was one in which CEOs, staffs, and trustees all played significant roles in holding their institutions in trust for the greater good of society. Servant leadership, like stewardship, assumes first and foremost a commitment to serving the needs of others. It also emphasizes the use of openness and persuasion, rather than control.
- *Commitment to the growth of people*: Servant leaders believe that people have an intrinsic value beyond their tangible contributions as workers. As such, the servant leader is deeply committed to the growth of each and every individual within his or her organization. The servant leader recognizes the tremendous responsibility to do everything in his or her power to nurture the personal and professional growth of employees and colleagues. In practice, this can include, but is not limited to, concrete actions such as making funds available for personal and professional development, taking a personal interest in the ideas and suggestions

from everyone, encouraging worker involvement in decision-making, and actively assisting laid-off employees to find other positions.
- *Building community*: The servant leader senses that much has been lost in recent human history as a result of the shift from local communities to large institutions as the primary shaper of human lives. This awareness causes the servant leader to seek to identify some means for building community among those who work within a given institution. Servant leadership suggests that true community can be created among those who work in businesses and other institutions. Greenleaf said, "All that is needed to rebuild community as a viable life form for large numbers of people is for enough servant leaders to show the way, not by mass movements, but by each servant leader demonstrating his or her unlimited liability for a quite specific community-related group."

These ten characteristics of servant leadership are by no means exhaustive. However, they serve to communicate the power and promise that this concept offers to servant leaders who are open to its invitation and challenge.

It is helpful to understand that servant leadership starts within each of us, and that it is primarily a personal philosophy and commitment that we can choose to practice in any environment. Also, servant leadership is not a "leadership style" that one puts on and takes off like a coat, depending upon the weather. Rather, if we understand Greenleaf's best test as the fundamental understanding of servant leadership, then it becomes clear that the choice to act as a servant leader is ours to make, and no one else. Personally, embracing servant leadership does not require the approval of the supervisor or the organization's chief executive. We don't need anyone's permission to personally do our best to act as a servant leader. It is our choice.

Another helpful insight is to state the obvious: There are no perfect servant leaders and no perfect servant-led institutions. Institutions are led by people, and people are imperfect. Even the most well-intentioned servant leaders will at some point in time do or say something we regret. At those times, the best thing to do is to sincerely apologize, and to seek to learn from it. In other instances, someone may become angry for a decision that we are convinced was the right one and made with the greater good in mind. When that happens, and if we are aware of it, the opportunity is there to try and promote healing by reaching out to one another. While there are no perfect servant leaders, through our ongoing development and practice, we can become *authentic* servant leaders. As the stories in this book suggest, the effective use of foresight, listening, and other servant leader characteristics is often at the heart of profoundly positive change within schools.

Servant leadership requires personal commitment and dedication. It is also a universal concept—one that we can recognize in ourselves, and in others, when we come to understand what it means, and what it looks like in practice.

In 2018, Michael J. Reilly and I wrote an essay titled, "Make Your Life Extraordinary: The Teacher as Servant-Leader" (*The International Journal of Servant-Leadership*, Vol. 12, 2018). In it, we looked at some of the ways in which teachers act as servant leaders in our lives. Among our conclusions was that a committed servant leader teacher creates a positive environment where a culture of sharing and caring dominate. The same thing is true of school principals who are servant leaders, who have an even greater possibility and responsibility for the creation of entire schools where servant leadership can take root and grow.

For many years, I have been both a friend and a fan of Rocky Wallace, and of his series of books on servant leadership and school principals. If inspired by what you have read here, I invite you to peruse his earlier books: *Principal to Principal: Conversations in Servant Leadership and School Transformation* (2008); *The Servant Leader and High School Change* (2009); *Breaking Away from the Corporate Model* (2009); and, *Servant Leadership: Leaving a Legacy* (2012). All are published by Rowman & Littlefield, and all are well worth reading for their own insights on the impact of school principals as servant leaders.

In *Service in the Trenches: School Principals Share True Stories of Servant Leadership,* Rocky Wallace, Stephanie Sullivan, Eve Proffitt, and their colleagues in Kentucky's University Principal Preparation Initiative have given all of us a great gift in bringing together so many significant stories of school principals as servant leaders—women and men who are helping to change the world for the better, one day at a time. I invite you to read what is contained within this book and to draw strength and inspiration from it for your own servant leader journey.

—Larry C. Spears
Servant-Leadership Scholar, Gonzaga University (Spokane)
Senior Advisory Editor, *The International Journal of Servant-Leadership*
President, The Spears Center for Servant-Leadership, Inc. (Indianapolis)
Author-Editor, *Insights on Leadership* and other books

Introduction

Lu Young

> *The servant leader is servant first . . . It begins with the natural feeling that one wants to serve, to serve first. The conscious choice brings one to aspire to lead . . . The difference manifests itself in the care taken by the servant—first to make sure that other people's highest priority needs are being served.*—Robert K. Greenleaf (1970, p. 6)

The catalyst for this book grew out of an earlier collaboration involving a team of educational leadership colleagues in Kentucky who came together to reflect on and write about the new Professional Standards for Educational Leaders (NPBEA, 2015) and the impact the new standards would have on leadership preparation across the Commonwealth. From that collaborative effort grew the desire to shine a light on some amazing principals who can aptly be described as *servant leaders*. Before we recount those stories, it is important to anchor them around a functional understanding of servant leadership as both theory and practice in P–12 schools and other organizations. When one first grapples with the term *servant leadership*, it may evoke some confusion or appear to be a contradiction because we often think of the roles of servants and leaders as opposite ends of a spectrum. "Many find it hard to accept the phenomenon of servant leadership because they do not understand how a servant can be a leader and how a leader can be a servant; that is, it seems to be an oxymoron" (Focht & Ponton, 2015, p. 44). They go on to point out that servant leaders may even understand "leading and serving as synonymous" (p. 44).

WHAT DO WE MEAN BY SERVANT LEADERSHIP?

Robert Greenleaf first coined the term *servant leader* in 1970, yet servant leadership still lacks a coherent, theoretical framework today (Parris & Peachey, 2013). For that reason, scholars across various fields have attempted to codify servant leadership and its characteristics for decades. Those efforts are helpful in that they begin to frame the kinds of behaviors and dispositions servant leaders are likely to embody. They also help those of us in higher education who work to build capacity among aspiring school leaders to better understand and illustrate servant leadership as a construct, grounded in the belief that such characteristics can be both *taught* and *learned* in leadership preparation programs.

Servant leadership has become a prominent and popular approach to leadership in the twenty-first century across a variety of public, private, and nonprofit sectors. In an attempt to better understand and assess the impact of servant leadership, Parris and Peachey (2013) identified and systematically examined a set of 39 empirical studies, a synthesis of which punctuated some key findings that shed light on the understanding and application of servant leadership. Those findings revealed that, despite a lack of commonly held consensus about the meaning of servant leadership, the philosophy of servant leadership is being practiced across a variety of contexts. Perhaps most importantly, they concluded that "servant leadership is a viable leadership theory that helps organizations and improves the well-being of followers" (Parris and Peachey, 2013, p. 377).

Also of interest to the readers of this book, Parris and Peachey (2013) noted that a significant percentage of the studies devoted to the exploration of servant leadership, 44 percent, occurred in educational settings. That finding does not come as a surprise to the author of this chapter because the tenets of servant leadership resonate naturally in school settings where leaders are particularly concerned with the well-being of their followers, students, and staff. It could, in fact, be argued that successful leadership in schools is almost entirely dependent upon the success of one's *followers*. Leadership dispositions like altruism and empathy, commitment to service, and concern for the community are themes that reverberate throughout the stories contained herein in much the same way these dispositions feature prominently throughout the Professional Standards for Educational Leaders (NPBEA, 2015).

SERVANT LEADERSHIP IN PRACTICE

Greenleaf (1998), a self-proclaimed student of organizations and how things get done, believed that the primary role of leadership was to meet the needs of others. Servant leaders focus on others, not themselves or their own self-interest (Greenleaf, 1970). Greenleaf describes "the best test" of servant leadership through these questions: "Do those served grow as persons? Do they, *while being served*, become healthier, wiser, freer, more autonomous, more likely themselves to become servants?" (1970, p. 6). Stone et al. (2003) accentuate the critical importance of the servant leader's focus on and investment in others, noting that "Servant leadership is a belief that organizational goals will be achieved on a long-term basis only by first facilitating the growth, development, and general well-being of the individuals who comprise the organization" (p. 5).

Larry Spears (2010), president and CEO of the Greenleaf Center for Servant-Leadership, offers an overview of an emerging approach to leadership that honors the duality of the terms, servant as leader, leader as servant. Spears builds on the foundation that the servant leader's focus is first and foremost on others. He goes on to identify ten central tenets of servant leadership that emerged out of his careful study of the work of Greenleaf. Those characteristics (Spears, 2010) are listening, empathy, healing, awareness, persuasion, conceptualization, foresight, stewardship, commitment to the growth of people, and building community.

The stories in this book illustrate servant leadership in action and many of the signature elements of servant leadership can be traced across these pages. These stories are deeply rooted in the reciprocal experiences of leaders and followers and they convey real challenges, emotions, accomplishments, and victories that inspire optimism and hope for a brighter future for our schools and communities and the servants who lead them.

REFERENCES

Focht, A., & Ponton, M. (2015). Identifying Primary Characteristics of Servant Leadership: 44 DELPHI STUDY. *International Journal of Leadership Studies*, 9(1), 44–61.

Greenleaf, R.K. (1970). The Servant as Leader. http://www.ediguys.net/Robert_K_Greenleaf_The_Servant_as_Leader.pdf

Greenleaf, R. K. (1998). *The power of servant-leadership: Essays*. Berrett-Koehler Publishers.

National Policy Board for Educational Administration (2015). Professional Standards for Educational Leaders 2015. Reston, VA: Author. https://www.npbea.org/wp

-content/uploads/2017/06/Professional-Standards-for-Educational-Leaders_2015.pdf

Parris, D. L., & Peachey, J. W. (2013). A Systematic Literature Review of Servant Leadership Theory in Organizational Contexts. *Journal of Business Ethics, 113*(No.3), 377–393.

Spears, L. (2010). Character and Servant Leadership: Ten Characteristics of Effective, Caring Leaders. *Journal of Virtues & Leadership, 1*(1).

Spears, L. (2005, August). *The understanding and practice of servant-leadership.* https://www.regent.edu/wp-content/uploads/2020/12/spears_practice.pdf

Stone, A.G., Russell, R., & Patterson K. (2003). Transformational versus servant leadership—A difference in leader focus. *Leadership and Organization Development Journal, 25*(4), 349–364. https://regent.edu/wp-content/uploads/2020/12/stone_transformation_versus.pdf

1

The Rookie

Rocky Wallace

The servant leader is much like a shepherd, standing in the gap—leading the flock toward home. —Rocky Wallace

John was hired on July 18, and the superintendent wanted him to begin his first day on the job the following morning. He could not contain his excitement as he drove home from the follow-up interview to share the good news with his wife. He was off to his first education leadership conference that very weekend, and she went shopping for him for new professional clothes.

The three weeks leading up to the opening day of school flew by, and John hoped he had prepared the school well for the fall term. The former principal had moved to the high school and had given him an hour "cram" tutorial on the school's culture, staff, and protocols.

FIRST DAY

John was up before daylight and wearing a new suit arrived at the school at dawn, just as the early morning buses began rolling in. He wanted to greet the students as they came off the buses, but soon realized the classroom doors all around the building were still locked. Come to find out, his day shift custodian had called in sick. John thought to himself: "You've got to be kidding me! My first day in my first year, and I have no custodian! If I could get my hands on him right now . . . "

John hurriedly went from room to room and learned quickly how to use his set of keys (on-the-job training for sure). As the staff began to show up, he greeted everyone and prepared for his first assembly in the gym. His new secretary (also her first year in the school office) helped as much as she could.

An August morning rain soon turned into a downpour, and as John entered the gym where a school full of students and adults were awaiting their new principal, he began to announce homeroom rosters, someone spoke up, "Can't hear you! Speak louder." Then someone else let him know that when it rained, the sound system in the gym often didn't work. The rest of the day went well—except for the realization that the former principal had often supervised lunchroom duty for his teachers.

FIRST WEEK

John loved his new work. He and his secretary were indeed overwhelmed, but the district office staff were patient, and so were his teachers. He spent lots of his days going back and forth to classrooms, checking on various needs and making sure the daily routine was running smoothly. One day, his secretary commented that his back was wet with sweat. (These were the days before email and text messaging).

But about two or three days into Week 1, a disgruntled father came bursting into John's office. "What is this note about my kids having head lice?"

"Well Sir, the district policy says . . ."

At that comment, the irate parent literally started to come across the desk. John's only instinctive reply was: "Now, if you're going to curse, we won't talk any further."

John was amazed—it worked. The man stopped, lowered his voice, and remained calm for the rest of the conversation, and left the office much more satisfied than when he had first arrived.

Also, in Week 1, John learned that the former principal had taken care of the payment of bills for the school. So, since the secretary was new too, John had no choice but to sit down on Friday and make sure everything had been accounted for financially, including preparing to balance the school's bank statement by month's end.

At home, John's wife and toddler daughter met him at the door each evening—often, well past dinner time. But his wife later said, "He came home late, but always with a smile on his face." John did love the work. It was never a dull moment and helping people every day in an array of circumstances came easy for him.

FIRST SEMESTER

As the late summer turned to fall, John could not believe how fast the weeks flew by. He did not remember even looking out his office window all semester because he was so busy. But he sunk back in his chair the morning he got the call that one of his mentor principals from his earlier years as a teacher had suddenly passed away. At the funeral visitation, he could not believe Ray was gone. He had been a one of a kind school leader—putting the kids and staff first in every way. John realized a lot of his school management tendencies and habits were from what he had learned from Ray, and he was honored to be exhibiting some of Ray's leadership characteristics.

The week of Thanksgiving, John decided to ride the buses on the p.m. routes so he could learn where the students lived. What an eye opener, as many of these homes (sometimes more like shacks) were off the beaten path—up lonely hollers on gravel roads. And many of these families lived in deep poverty. It was no wonder few of these kids were involved in sports and other after-school activities. The drive to the school's location was such a long way.

John envisioned an intramural league, where parents would coach and every student who wanted to participate was put on a team—and played. This dream became a reality in years two and three—Friday night basketball at the school. The community loved it, especially the students who would have normally never had the opportunity to dress out in uniform on a school team.

FIRST YEAR

As the year rolled on, one of the school's classified staff became increasingly impatient with how the school district was meeting the needs of her handicapped grandchild, who attended John's school. John realized he was in the middle of potential litigation against the school and district, as the Admissions and Release Committee meetings dragged out what could have been a simple solution—simply purchase a special swing for the playground. Fortunately, the district agreed to provide the needed financial support for the swing. Sitting at the table and showing compassion, the issue was resolved.

Wintertime brought snow days and an opportunity to catch up at the school when students and staff were at home. John noticed he was feeling "butterflies" in his stomach much of the time—nervous worry as the reality of being a first-year principal at a K–8 rural school brought with it various attitudes from the staff. One group loved his "If it's a fresh idea, let's do it" belief in giving everyone new beginnings; but another group missed the tradition and established processes of the former administration.

A new counselor had been hired and was shared with the high school. John turned the in-school suspension program over to her, and her innovative ideas for working with the problem kids were not always supported by the staff. It was no one's fault—simply the complexities of adults working together in a pressure environment where they are responsible for the welfare of hundreds of students, daylight to sundown every day.

At the end of spring term, a house fire took the lives of some children in the county, who were relatives of an 8th grade student in John's school. At the 8th grade graduation, John dug deep to give one of the best talks he had delivered in his entire career. He honored this family and shared that the whole school grieved with them. John realized then that this job was so much more than supervising the day-to-day operations of the school. Added to these responsibilities was the need for authentic relationship with all stakeholders—care, trust, growing together as a school community, both on the good days and bad.

In the years to follow, John did indeed grow into the role of servant leader. He embraced innovation, giving all staff room to fail; thus, room to grow. He took kids who were sick and stranded at school in the middle of the day home in his personal vehicle because no one at home could get to the school at that hour of the day. Yes, risky, but the right thing to do. He advocated for the school at school board meetings, and yes, became good friends with the custodian who called in sick on his first day, and became a huge advocate for all his classified staff. Simply put, he fell in love with the little rural community that had trusted him as a rookie principal and believed in his focus on a culture of care.

THE TIME FLIES BY

After year three, a school where he had taught just a few years earlier as a teacher came calling, and later that summer he took the offer. But the decision was not without pain, as John's "heart of hearts" hurt for weeks as he walked away from those who he had grown to love in the little school in the country that gave him his chance to be a principal. Now, decades later, he still looks back with memories that remind him what it means to be a servant leader, and he realizes that perhaps his earliest years as a principal were his best, as he let his core value of "people over management" define the "rookie." And that had been good enough . . . Perhaps even his finest hour in his long and blessed journey as an educator.

QUESTIONS FOR REFLECTION

- Why is it important to go beyond what is mandated in serving/growing an effective school?
- Why are the ideas from stakeholders so important when a leader first begins serving an organization?
- Why does a "culture of care" take priority over other organizational strategy/processes?

FURTHER READING

Brooks, D. (2020). *The second mountain.* New York: Random House.

2

The Substitute

Mike Hylen

Leadership is not a position we attain, it is a disposition we exhibit.—
Mike Hylen

ANSWERING THE CALL

Bill had just settled into his office chair from breakfast duty in the cafeteria when the phone rang. It was central office. The social studies teacher had called in sick and the school was unable to fill his classroom with a substitute. The principal was not surprised. This was not the first time. Leading a charter school, whose student body was comprised predominantly of students expelled from the local public school system and many active gang members, made it difficult to build a list of quality substitutes. On top of that, the location of the school made it undesirable for some.

If need be, Bill knew there was a person or two he could call who had been willing to previously serve as a substitute. However, observations of the individuals suggested they were less than ideal—even if just filling a room for a day. He knew the students needed more than just a warm body in the room, so the only option at this point was for him to serve as the substitute for the day. It made sense, since the students knew him and had come to trust him as their principal and leader.

With the decision made, Bill informed central office and his teachers in the building he would not be readily accessible due to this commitment. His class could only be interrupted if an egregious act had been committed. His students deserved his full attention and consideration. These students were used to being slighted by teachers and school leaders, and he wanted to show them he held them in the same esteem as all other students. He had worked hard to build a positive relationship with them, and he did not want anything to set that back.

Arriving in the classroom that day, Bill knew during the very first period this might be a particularly awkward task. He knew he could handle the classroom and was familiar with the content being taught, so that did not cause any hesitation. The awkwardness came as a result of the setting. The students were studying the Civil Rights movement and on this particular day would be watching a video about the sit-in movement followed by a discussion of the topic. Again, in and of itself, this was not a difficult task. Yet, being Caucasian and leading four classes of a 100 percent African American student body on this topic made him a little uncomfortable.

With this knowledge in hand, Bill found himself glad it was he leading the classroom that day. He could only imagine what may be the case if it had been someone with whom the students were not familiar. The one thing of which he was certain was that his relationship with the students made this possible. He had come to learn that they were open, honest, and forthright with adults, and any adult who responded the same way with them earned their respect. He knew being open to wherever the discussion may lead would go a long way with his students. With that understanding in place, he settled in.

BUILDING TRUSTING RELATIONSHIPS

One cannot assume that students come to school willing to fully trust adults. This is especially true in a charter school where the majority of students have had negative experiences in previous school settings or come from homes with an abusive parent or adult. Bill was mindful of this and knew his first course of action when accepting the position was to build student trust. The challenge was that building trust takes work. He also knew that building trusting relationships required four key elements: consistency, compassion, communication, and competency.

Consistency is easily the most understandable of these elements in building trust. Students feel comfortable with adults who consistently respond to them in a positive manner. They come to trust them more readily. Similarly, competency is readily understandable. If a student does not believe a person can perform a task, he or she will not trust the person to complete a task or request.

What about communication and compassion? According to Stephen Covey, "Trust is . . . the most essential ingredient in effective communication" (1994). Yet, open and honest communication is essential in building trust. As such, it becomes a cyclical matter; one that requires an open line allowing students to communicate with openness and honesty without fear of rejection. This may be the biggest obstacle all of us face with being open and honest . . . fear of rejection. A process must be in place for transparent communication. This is accomplished by being available to students outside of the four office walls, so that conversations inside them are meaningful and effective.

As for compassion, one would think this would not be an issue. By nature, educators are extremely caring and giving of themselves. Yet, how would Bill be able to demonstrate compassion when many of his interactions with individuals occurred as a result of a disciplinary write up? Students may not see the principal as compassionate while he or she is applying strict consequences. The answer was simple. Bill had to ensure that any disciplinary action focused on correcting the negative behavior and that he was understanding of the student's emotion at the time. By communicating it was not an indictment of the student, but rather a means for addressing a poor behavior choice, it was easier to earn their trust.

Building student trust takes time. It is a gradual process. While younger students may come to school with a sense of trust in their teachers, older ones may be a little more hesitant due to life experiences. As such, educators must be patient and not expect too much too soon. Additionally, the educator must be slow in establishing rapport with the students and being vulnerable, so not to overwhelm them during the process.

A LESSON FROM THE STUDENTS

Having built a culture of trust in his school, Bill entered the classroom. The first period bell rang and immediately he took to the task at hand. A quick check of attendance, and it was time to start the video. From the start, he could tell it struck a nerve with his students. There on the screen were black students being trained in a church to enter all-white restaurants and sit at counters where they were not permitted. White volunteers were asked to serve the role of combatants as part of the preparation. Their job was to yell loudly, curse at, and even throw food at those conducting the sit-in, while the black students practiced sitting quietly and peacefully.

During this first period, there were comments from students. For the most part, they remained attentive and their responses did lack some of the emotion Bill had feared. Still, he sat and observed, looking for anything that may signal the need to turn off the video. There was no need at this point. To say the least, keeping the students engaged was not a challenge with this activity. Bill wished all the classes he had taught when a teacher had this level of engagement.

The time came on the video when those participating in the sit-ins left the confines of the church and paraded down to restaurants filled with white consumers. The participants included both black and white students, giving Bill some sense of ease for what the conversation may entail after the video. He watched as the emotions of his students began to rise. The actions that they were witnessing seemed much harsher than what was observed during the practice sessions. It almost seemed to Bill that some of his students were responding as if they could relate to such events.

When it was time to stop the video and start a discussion with the students, Bill was surprised at how maturely the students conducted themselves, despite their high emotions. Overall, he felt at ease with the conversation and felt comfortable asking clarifying questions, something he thought he might be hesitant to do. Still, he was caught off guard with the response of one of his male students. The student simply stated, "Doc, you can't understand, you're not white." Bill, being of European dissent, was surprised by the student's statement and unaware of how to respond, so he left it alone.

The day seemed to go by quickly after that. To Bill's surprise, it ended without incident. He was happy for it to be over. Yet, something about the student's statement about Bill's "color blindness" caused him to sit and ponder in his office long after all others were gone for the day. It became clear to him he had an incorrect understanding of the students' perspective of race. The students did not see the color of his skin, rather the matter of his heart. White was a construct to them, not a color, hence, it was easy for them to trust in their principal.

Looking back over the day's activities, Bill knew he had made the right choice to serve as a substitute, even if it meant getting behind in other tasks needing to be accomplished. He had learned more from his students that day than they did from him, due to his willingness to fill a void and serve his students in a different way. All as a result of being a servant leader.

QUESTIONS FOR REFLECTION

- Was it a good choice for the principal to leave his post for a day to serve as a substitute? Why or why not?
- What positive character traits did he portray, and what was the impact?
- Why is it important for a servant leader to build trusting relationships?

FURTHER READING

Covey, S. (1994). *First Things First*.
Singleton, G., & Singleton, C. (2006). *Courageous Conversations About Race.*

3

Sacrifices

Carol Christian

As a budding leader, don't get hung up on the title of principal or whatever level of leadership you have attained. You may just find yourself being the janitor, the bus driver, the nurse and detective, babysitter or the parent to name just a few. Whatever your title, remember it is all for the good of the kids we serve.—Carol Christian

When Sandy left the classroom to become a principal, she found out during district orientation that all administrators had to be certified to drive a bus. She certainly thought someone in the central office had made a mistake as she was the new principal, not a bus driver. But they were correct. All administrators had to be able to drive a bus in case the district experienced a shortage of bus drivers.

At the end of the weeklong training, Sandy's stomach churned, knowing that she had to pass the Commercial Driver's License test and actually drive a bus on the highway. She thought, "If I could only announce on the radio, if you see a blonde driving a big yellow bus on route 68 around 10:00 a.m., get out of the way!" That experience taught her to respect those who did drive the buses on a regular basis. It gained her great respect among the bus drivers as she constantly shared her appreciation of them. It was a painful, yet valuable, lesson to walk in someone else's shoes.

On another wild and crazy day in the life of an administrator Sandy arrived at school before the kids and most staff had arrived. The janitor approached her, sharing that the sink on the third floor was overflowing. Also, he had gotten a call from the lunchroom manager that the dishwasher was broken. And, he had been radioed that bus 22 would be on campus in 10 minutes and they wanted an administrator to meet them out back (typically an indication that something was not good and must be dealt with regarding student misbehavior on the bus).

Not even in her office yet, but entering the secretary's office, the phones were ringing off the hook. Upon answering, Sandy was informed that a wreck had occurred, and four teachers would be late because traffic was backed up until things were cleared. Sandy kicked into Plan B with getting coverage for those teachers' classes. Reaching her office, she answered the phone to be informed she was three subs short that morning. It was then that she realized it was going to be a great day: sink overflowing, dishwasher down, meet bus 22, and seven classrooms to be covered.

Plus, the news reported there might be a snowstorm coming in around 10:00 a.m. that morning! Sandy prayed to get through the day. She helped the janitor mop the water off the 3rd floor, and her Dad being a plumber, she knew a little about plumbing and was able to identify the problem in the lunchroom with the dishwasher and ensure it was repaired and working properly.

The snowstorm did arrive—not at 10:00 a.m. but as the cafeteria was filled with students eating! There was a flurry of announcements to get students on buses. The ice came before the snow. Phones were ringing nonstop, and parents were jamming the office. Sandy was suddenly called outside to assist a parent who had fallen, resulting in a compound fracture of her lower leg. Sandy calmed the parent, stabilized the leg, and provided her a blanket until the ambulance arrived.

Down the hall from the office, a 6th grader had thrown up. The janitors were on their own mission to get the sidewalks safe and cleared. Sandy had no other options but to clean up the mess. Choking back the urge to heave herself, she managed to complete the task.

Running through the office, the secretary told Sandy she needed to talk to her. "Not now, I am in a hurry." Backing up into the office Sandy exclaimed, "Why is a TV station in our building?" The secretary said, "I tried to warn you. They want to follow a principal in a weather crisis!!!"

Eventually, the day ended. Kids were home safe. Sandy was found at home staring at a wall and babbling. In one short morning as a principal, a plumber, a nurse, a janitor, a bus driver, and a TV celebrity had all needed her undivided attention.

Sandy thought, "Sometimes, you just have to do what you have to do in situational leadership as one who serves." She did not think there was much she could not handle as a result of these experiences, and commented to herself that "I need to keep a journal of these days, and some day (maybe not today), I will look back and enjoy a good belly laugh!"

QUESTIONS FOR REFLECTION

- Why is it important for a school principal to ensure a healthy work/life balance?
- Why is it important for a school principal to have high emotional intelligence?
- Why is it important for a school principal to be proactive in addressing potential issues that could surface?

FURTHER READING

Goleman, D. (2005). *Emotional Intelligence: Why It Can Matter More Than IQ*. New York: Random House.

4

From Darkness to Light

Josh Gupton

A man must be big enough to admit his mistakes, smart enough to profit from them, and strong enough to correct them.—John C. Maxwell

As the new assistant principal stood in the vacant office with white walls, two large windows, and a paper label next to his door printed with his name, he was a very proud man. Just days before, Steve would have never believed he would be standing there. The previous weeks of his life were a whirlwind of activity that would define his future within the school district. More importantly, the man he would become would impact his future relationship with family, friends, and staff. Pride quickly turned to fear and nervousness once reality occurred. Ten long years as a music educator and two short years in counseling were nothing compared to the mountain he was about to climb.

Steve did not always desire to be in administration, because for years he had observed the immense stress placed on school leaders. However, he knew that this opportunity would be the only way to work more efficiently one-on-one with students in his building he knew could benefit from his counseling experience.

As a counselor, the administration only allowed Steve a short block of time to meet with students before completing the daily music education rotation. The opportunity for advancement came when the "district shuffle" had occurred over the summer. Several administrators had received new roles, his school had just hired a new principal, and the assistant was moving to another school. Steve recognized a brilliant opportunity. If he could land the job, he could pursue more avenues to serve students through counseling while also attending to the school's needs as an administrator.

After several phone calls to the former administration, trusted friends, and close peers, all agreed Steve would be a good candidate for the role. A long and nervous week went by while he anxiously awaited to hear any news. Steve prayed that the seat would be his if it were God's will. One day, the phone rang, and the next thing he knew, the meeting was scheduled with the new administration.

On the interview day, Steve arrived early, and Mrs. Mary, the new principal, greeted him at the door. She was delighted to see that Steve had applied and ushered him into the library. He met a few other district staff, who had questions about ethics, experience, future desires, and so on. Steve met each with the best answer he could deliver. Shortly after leaving, feeling very apprehensive about his chances, the call came. On the other end, Mrs. Mary congratulated Steve on being the new assistant principal. She explained that due to being new to administration, he would need to complete his administration degree within two years. Although a daunting task, he readily agreed.

THE ROOKIE

Steve eventually enrolled in a program at a local university. Although he had full faith in his new boss, he had minimal confidence in himself. He had only spoken a few times with the administration about their jobs and honestly didn't know where to even begin. On the first day, Mrs. Mary started working on several items busily in her office. Her first task for Steve was to create a daily schedule for each grade and update the intervention program guidelines for low-achieving students. Immediately, Steve began to panic. He didn't want to disappoint in his very first assignments.

Slowly walking back to his new office, he sat down to think. By the end of the day, he had updated the previous year's schedule and intervention policies and redesigned them to fit the upcoming year. The documents had everything a shining progressive school would need. With Mary's approval, he emailed them out to the staff with a smile on his face. Within moments the calls, emails, and texts began to roll in. A flood of disapproval washed across the office. He had failed in only a few hours, and it was apparent that everyone had little faith in his abilities.

The next day Mrs. Mary approached Steve and explained that sometimes you just have to stand your ground and try things out. With slightly renewed hope, Steve worked in some of the suggestions from staff and explained how this would be the schedule the school would follow. Even though the staff didn't foresee his pushback, Steve stood firm. In addition to scheduling and interventions, he developed several more policies addressing discipline, attendance updates, budget decisions, and transportation lists. Every step taken forward met stark resistance. Still, he was given these tasks and was determined to make the best of what he knew was right.

Mrs. Mary gave him confidence and was the wind to his sails. However, Steve found himself completely overwhelmed before the school opened its doors for fall term. Within the first week on the job that summer, he felt as though he was doing the work of an army. Staff that had worked with him for years now seemed to be gathering forces against every move he made. There were too many tasks to focus intently on all of them. So, Steve's goal at the moment was to keep the school going, and perfection would have to wait.

DYSFUNCTION

Opening day for staff was met with few smiles and many stern faces. Mrs. Mary's opening speech to the staff was firm on the foundation that we would work together and move this school forward to be the best in the district. Steve stood by her but feeling that something wasn't right about the entire day. Staff members took to their rooms and prepared to follow the new master schedule and other details provided to them. Truthfully, Steve thought he and Mrs. Mary were on the verge of witnessing a massive train wreck.

As students stepped off the bus on their first day, the staff greeted them with smiles and stickers. Everyone met in the gym for the morning meeting while the new school motto was displayed widely for all students and staff to see. As Steve stood in front of the student body, he could see every teacher putting on their best faces for the students. Classes were called down from the bleachers, students lined up ready to go, and so began the long-awaited start of fall term.

As the day progressed, there was confusion about overlapping classes, schedules failing, and disgruntlement from every corner. By the end of the week, staff was utterly fed up with programs, operations, and the plan, which had been changed so many times. It was like a thousand-piece puzzle with five hundred pieces missing. Nothing was working, and the assistance from Mrs. Mary was not helping fix what was now fully considered Steve's problem. He had been yelled at by staff, brushed off by those he knew best, and given the silent treatment when he walked past them.

Upon the end of the first week, Steve, the once-proud assistant principal, now went home and wept. His family could do nothing but offer a shoulder on which to cry, but he seemed too distant and embarrassed to accept their support. After the first few months in the administration role he had so wanted, they noticed he was no longer the eager and happy person he once was. If this was the beginning, what did the future have to offer?

The coming weeks came with the same frustrations and troubles as the past. Steve couldn't balance all the work. On top of it all, many discipline issues came rolling into his office. Each one presented its own unique challenge. There were accounts of cheating, fights, bullying, stealing, bus issues, and so much more. Steve listened to each complaint and addressed each student with what he thought was right. Not knowing how to compose a policy, Steve kept using the current discipline guide, which was vague. Teachers were becoming upset because he gave different students committing the same transgressions varied punishments.

Steve thought he was listening and counseling the students to do better. He knew that this was the right path to take. Counseling was what he was meant to do and blending his new empowered role with the experience of his past could only end in a better school. Unbeknownst to him, this was not working at all. Repeat offenders became the norm, new issues appeared daily, and the office was flooded with complaints. He just added this to the top of his list of failures for the year. It was his burden to carry and speaking to his boss would only repeat the now broken record constantly playing in his head.

Whispers from staff showed that students were not making gains. Intervention data showed students sinking lower than ever. Student, as well as teacher morale, was at an all-time low. Reading classes were overwhelmed with low levels, and math growth dropped rapidly. When Steve walked into classes, he could see the self-confidence drain from students' faces. Most were giving up, and teachers were left with few options from Steve's "glorious" plan.

MENTORING

Steve began looking everywhere for an answer. He traveled to different schools to view their programs and looked within his own school's walls for the answers. But every effort was nullified at each turn. In his mind, there was now a clear picture that he could not be a leader, and termination was in his future. What he didn't see was that hope was on the horizon. Through his classes, he had begun learning about being a leader and serving others. Through God's grace, Dr. Ron, a professor for the university, was assigned to Steve for mentorship. As the weeks progressed, Dr. Ron spoke about servant leadership, becoming a steward toward others, and using your role to help others succeed. This was all a new perspective for Steve.

Every time he spoke with Dr. Ron, he compared what was happening at his school against what healthy school culture looked like. Week after week, the conversations became more meaningful. Dr. Ron listened and gave sound, straightforward advice—noticing progress along the way. He began guiding

Steve towards making better decisions based on the principles of servant leadership. Since the job was his, Steve could see a beacon of hope for the first time. In truth, he had decided to leave this job, until he found faith after conversations with his new mentor. Little did Dr. Ron know how much his mentoring placement saved Steve from feeling as if the whole year was a failure.

Steve knew he needed to make a major decision. Should he continue to be firm and look to himself and external sources to lead his school, or should he transform into the person he knew he needed to be and move away from his principal's advice? Through prayer, family, and his trusted mentor, Steve decided a change must take place, or he was going to lose everything in his work life he knew God had placed before him. This change would not be an easy path because of the mindset developed across the building. To accomplish this new beginning, a paradigm shift had to occur, and it was already past the middle of the year. (Not to mention, Steve was about to eat a large slice of humble pie.)

The next day, Steve stood tall as he entered the building and greeted everyone he saw. Instead of staying in his office, he visited classrooms throughout the day and started building back relationships with his staff by asking how they truly felt. He brought in staff for the reading programs and intervention classes to recommend improvements and build the program from scratch. He communicated with grade levels to create a schedule that fit their needs. Steve saw a sense of empowerment flow over his staff. As Steve brought others on board and into leadership roles, he noticed an improvement in his life. Work at school, and time with his family at home, was better. In addition, the staff was willing to offer suggestions and share their skills with him. He was not alone in his office anymore trying to do it all.

With renewed efforts, success and growth had now taken hold of the intervention plan. Although it was not perfect, the newly formed team had made a new diverse plan that leveled all students. New materials were being used that were on each student's level. Slowly, progress was being achieved. Students celebrated their achievements as they moved forward. An updated library schedule allowed students to check out books throughout various times of the day to excel in their reading goals. Teachers were noticing tremendous changes in students' self-confidence. Although Steve still had a long way to go, things were looking better.

SELFISH LEADERSHIP

Steve now realized what he had thought was trust and good relations from his principal was all a facade of delegated tasks. He felt betrayed and could see as the staff began to build back, Mrs. Mary began to change as well. As staff trusted and came to him, it began to upset her. Soon, he started to see things take place that he had hoped wouldn't happen. His relations with his mentor, staff, and family began to mend themselves little by little, but Mrs. Mary seemed not to want to be around him anymore. During the last week of school, the day of reckoning came.

The following week saw extra meetings being held with the district superintendent, and the principal was nowhere to be found. Steve experienced more days where he was left to run operations while Mrs. Mary was absent. He became so concerned that he called the superintendent and asked whether his job was in trouble. The answer was to remain patient. Unfortunately, this was not the answer he wanted to hear. It appears all the progress made would once again be destroyed. That was not acceptable for him this near the end of the school year.

The principal's office was closed on the last day of the spring term, although Mrs. Mary occupied it. The day went well as teachers were finally happy, while still maintaining a tremendous amount of hesitance towards Steve as they wondered what would happen next. Mrs. Mary finally came out of her office and approached Steve, telling him she would not be in the building after that day. The now battle-worn Steve took a few days to wrap up what he could and left. By this time, he knew he would still have a job, but had no clue what the future would hold. Once again, help was on the way.

AUTHENTIC LEADERSHIP

As Steve started work the coming year, preparations were being made for the new principal. Teachers were buzzing the months before school opened about who would fulfill the role of their new leader. Truthfully, several were glad to see Steve remain in his role, making his heart happy. The announcement soon came that Mrs. Beth would be filling the lead position and a thousand unanswered questions went through his mind. He had heard very little about her. One staff member said that based on her former experience, she would snap the building back into shape. Several people said she was very strict and led with a firm hand. Steve had flashbacks of the previous year going through his mind, and he just wanted to cry.

The first workday came for Mrs. Beth, and as Steve entered the building, he was trying to seek out any new information before greeting her. He finally knocked on the door and was met with a pleasant greeting. She explained that she knew about everything that had happened previously and even shared information with him that he had not known. This answered a lot of reasons why the staff was acting the way they did towards him the past year. She went on to say that a lot of work Steve did was not his responsibility but was the principal's role. She was there to provide help, work in unity, bring the school's culture back together, and progress everyone forward from this point on. Steve had never felt better. He now had not one but two trusted mentors by his side.

There was still one major hurdle to overcome. Mrs. Beth explained to Steve that he had many relationships that were still very rocky from the destruction that happened with the last principal. It would be up to him to reinstate the lost trust and respect. The rest of that week, Mrs. Beth helped Steve improve the intervention and discipline policies that needed revisions and spoke to him about the inconsistent discipline from the past year. This would be his primary task in preparing for the new school year. He now knew what he needed to do to make things right and had a plan ready to go.

HEALTHY CULTURE, HEALTHY SCHOOL

Opening day had once again arrived, but this one was very different. Steve was to lead by example for both students and staff. And, relationships should be built beyond the workplace to truly connect with students and staff. It wasn't about leading by power, but to lead by *empowering others*. Consistency with policies and follow through was key to gaining trust and respect. Together, as a community, the school would grow into its strengths as a cohesive team. This year was going to be different.

Steve stood beside Mrs. Beth as she introduced herself and made opening day remarks. She then looked at him, nodded, and Steve stepped forward and began speaking. He admitted that he had made more mistakes than he ever imagined. He spoke of how he understood what being a servant leader meant by the end of the past year and apologized for taking so long to understand. He spoke of the wrongs he had already corrected and how he desired to move forward, building back better under the stewardship of Mrs. Beth. He finished by saying he hoped they would give him a chance to renew what was lost and prove that he could be a strong leader. There wasn't a round of applause or standing ovation, but Steve knew that they had always been there for him. Truthfully, his school family was why he was standing before them that day.

Through grace, Steve was given a second chance. He had the opportunity to learn to be humble and that growth through mistakes is okay for leaders. Learning to be a servant leader takes practice. Steve never gave up. Instead, he eventually witnessed increasing success and health for his school and family. Dr. Ron and Mrs. Beth helped Steve learn the foundation and principles of servant leadership and how to address challenging opportunities. He learned the importance of students and staff being involved in decision-making, and how a culture of care is paramount to the health and well-being of the school. In the end, he became the person he wanted to be and the leader the school needed him to be.

QUESTIONS FOR REFLECTION

- What do you believe was Steve's greatest hindrance in leadership during the first year of administration? How did this impact students at the school?
- Why is it essential to build relationships beyond the workplace walls to be a more effective servant leader? How would this help students and staff alike?
- Steve steadily gained self-awareness of his strengths and weaknesses. How would his new knowledge allow him to be a better servant leader to all?

FURTHER READING

Batterson, M. (2016). *In a Pit with a Lion on a Snowy Day: How to Survive and Thrive When Opportunity Roars.* Colorado Springs: Multnomah.

5

Pipeline

Jason Detre

Every hire is a multimillion dollar investment—treat them as such.— Jason Detre

Don had recently taken his second principal position. His first stint as a building-level principal had been successful by all measures. Teacher morale, staff retention, student test scores, and the overall school culture had changed under his leadership. As a result of his success, he had been recruited to take over a larger, and historically successful, school in a neighboring district.

Don had learned about an upcoming leadership workshop sponsored by his state administrative organization. His superintendent agreed to send him with a team from the district to this professional development opportunity, which was being led by Dr. Todd Whitaker. Whitaker gave Don much to mull over on his drive home and he used the two-hour trip to organize his thoughts.

After church on Sundays, Don often took advantage of the afternoon to put in a few uninterrupted hours at the school. This Sunday, he was focused on the recent leadership workshop. He pulled up a spreadsheet and began working. His task was to review his staff: their certifications, years of experience, and potential vacancies within the building. Don made a few projections and made an outline of how they might be implemented in his school.

Don understood that his plan was only a projection at this point. He had been around school long enough to understand that moves, career advancements, and other items were not always as predictable. Overall, he felt good about the information he had gathered.

CROCK POTTING

At 9:00 a.m. the following Monday, Don met with his leadership team to share his forecasting, which provided a clear picture of the potential vacancies within the school over the next few years. Jim, the assistant principal and a 20-year veteran in education, studied the chart. He was quick to point out a few teachers he thought the district would soon target for leadership positions.

Meanwhile, Jill, the guidance counselor, addressed the elephant in the room, "In the next three years, we could potentially lose the entire science department and most of the math department." Don asked, "So what do we do about it?" He had learned long ago to gather input from his team and to formulate a plan together. As the principal, he also knew that his opinion carried with it a lot of weight, so he generally waited to provide his ideas on a matter.

The team understood the educational landscape. The fact that colleges and universities were graduating fewer science and math teachers was not a foreign concept. Don and his team understood that their sleepy little rural town could be a tough sell for those who had just graduated college. Teaching vacancies in those areas were abundant across the Commonwealth and all the surrounding states. Teacher candidates could be selective on what positions they accepted.

The team finally centered on a discussion about recruitment. "We have to be able to sell our school, our district, and our community to potential employees," Jill summarized. Jim agreed with the team and he began to steer the conversation toward student teachers. This was a chord that had struck with Don since the Todd Whitaker professional learning. He shared with his team the professional learning insights he had gained, gave the group some homework, and settled on the next Monday morning for a follow-up meeting.

FOLLOWING THROUGH

The plan took shape and by October of that school year implementation began.

Jim, the assistant principal, had identified all the colleges and universities that serviced their region. He also created a document with contact information for each university's education department, placement person, math department head, and science department head. Jill, the guidance counselor, identified all faculty who were eligible to supervise student teachers based on rank, experience, and state guidelines.

Don emailed each of the university contacts to introduce himself and his administrative team. Next, he and Jim called each of the contacts to further develop relationships with those individuals. This was a specific strategy Don had picked up from his day with Todd Whitaker. He and his team spoke to eligible teachers about accepting student teachers over the next several years. Most of the staff was receptive. The plan began to take shape.

Don also spoke at two of the local colleges and sent a video message to potential student teachers at a few of the universities. He made a concentrated effort to recruit student teachers, attend job fairs, and ensure the school had applicants for any vacancy that might occur. Don, Jim, and Jill personally met with each new student teacher in the building, as the administrative team began to implement the new plan.

And for the upcoming year, the school had one vacancy. Guess who filled the job? A student teacher! Don had invested time in this young woman and had seen her grow as an educator. After informally and formally observing her teach, Don knew to:

- Make contacts and build relationships with local universities and colleges.
- Make new teacher placements with the best faculty mentors in the building.
- Meet with every student teacher, and always give them a welcome basket.
- Observe student teachers both formally and informally.
- Place student teachers on a schedule with other master teachers in the building, with a specific observation purpose.
- Build a relationship with each student teacher.
- Conduct mock interview with student teachers.

WORKING THE PLAN

Don and his team made this induction model a common practice during his tenure at the school. Student teachers in the building had a high success rate of landing a teaching position the following year.

Example: Tim, a student teacher in the math department, had difficulties at the start of his student teaching. He specifically struggled with student engagement and lesson planning. Don and his team could have easily dismissed Tim and not invested time and resources in him. But that was not Don's style. He believed in developing and investing in people. He engaged Tim's cooperating teacher, instructional coaches, and the administrative team to further support Tim.

At first, the young teacher was a little resistant to the coaching and seemed to almost take it personally, which prompted a one-on-one conversation with Don. Through this initial meeting, he had learned about Tim's background as a high school athlete. The new information allowed him to frame the conversation. He talked with Tim about coaching athletes and what a good coach does to make them better. He then talked about educational coaching and how it translates to improved practice in the classroom. Don also shared some of his struggles during his student teaching and reassured Tim that if he would be open to coaching, he would see growth.

Tim finished his student teaching, participated in the mock interview, and applied for a position in a neighboring district. Don did not have a math position open that school year but had been impressed with Tim's turn-around. Don realized the importance of developing the potential in others by promoting professional learning, regardless of where they would eventually be employed.

QUESTIONS FOR REFLECTION

- How are student teachers recruited in your school/district?
- What is your role as an administrator to develop student teachers in the area of classroom management, instruction, and pedagogy development?
- How can you invest in your teachers in year one, two, and year twenty-seven?

FURTHER READING

Whitaker, T. (2003). *What Great Principals Do Differently: Fifteen Things That Matter Most.* Larchment, NY: Eye on Education.

6

An Unlikely Administrator

Whitney Shannon Wilson

> *But among you, it will be different. Whoever wants to be a leader among you must be your servant.*—Matthew 20:26

Working in a school library had been Ashley's dream as a college student. The dream became a reality when she was hired to be the media specialist at the middle school in her hometown. The principal offered her every opportunity to build a great library program, and she worked tirelessly to make it the center of the school. She enjoyed significant success from touching the hearts of students to winning several grants to help improve the resource collection. Ashley was sure this was what she was meant to do—working with others to build a love for reading was her passion.

After serving as a librarian in her school for several years, the principal who had hired Ashley was promoted to the district office, and a search for a new principal began. Several applicants were interviewed, and a local, promising, and ambitious young man was selected. Ashley knew her new leader had a solid vision and had rallied her peers from day one to work with him to positively impact students. She assisted him on the school's leadership team and on other district committees to make their school one of the best in the area. In August of that year, she also discovered that she was expecting a little girl.

Having a new boss and a new baby brought on a new challenge, but Ashley was up for it. She had been given a new perspective because she now had her own daughter who would one day be a student in her school. The school enjoyed great success over the next year under new leadership, and the culture had also improved dramatically.

"We need to talk," her principal said, as he came into the library between class changes. Ashley wasn't sure what to make of this, but a sense of dread enveloped her after she considered his words. "Have you ever thought about moving downstairs?" Processing this question, Ashley wasn't sure what to make of the comment. She knew that downstairs meant the principal's office, but there wasn't anything that she could do "downstairs" because all the positions at the school were filled. He went on to explain that there were going to be some district moves, and the position of assistant principal would come open in their school.

"I don't know. I just really want to be the librarian here; I love my job. Plus, I have a baby at home. I don't think I am cut out for the responsibility of being an administrator," Ashley explained. Watching him think about these words, she wasn't sure if he accepted her answer. "Just remember why you do what you do. You can have a much larger impact from that chair (pointing downstairs) than you can in that one." He was now pointing at the old library chair sitting at the circulation desk. "Think about it—you have time to make a decision. This is what you were made to do, even if you don't think it is. Being a leader is your calling."

Ashley thought a lot about this conversation as the school year ended and the students left for summer vacation. Working in the library and reflecting upon her time in that space, she knew that her principal was right. Her impact on her community and her students as an administrator would be far-reaching.

THE FIRST YEAR

Prior to school starting, Ashley accepted the job as assistant principal in her school. Taking on this new role, she began handling student discipline and working on curriculum issues. The first year was hard since some students had a reputation for having challenging behaviors. Being a librarian, Ashley had never had to deal with the extremes of student behavior in this manner. Not only were the students a lot to handle, but there were multiple parents from this same group who also proved to be difficult.

As bad as some of the students were, some of them really needed Ashley. Some felt very comfortable confiding in her and allowing her to help them work through complicated situations that middle schoolers face. And, those students were the ones that kept her going in the new and challenging role she played.

Before the first year ended, Ashley was sure she had made a mistake. She even told her principal that she thought that she wanted to go back to the library. Ashley felt that she was not equipped for the position. Her principal encouraged her to continue in the position a few more months and promised that if she still did not like it after the second year, he would reassign her to her previous position.

That summer Ashley worked tirelessly to redo systems that had been adopted by the previous administration. Lunch schedules were adjusted; the master schedule was changed to reflect the vision and mission of the school; student dismissal was changed; and the discipline policy was updated. She also attended professional development and conferences over the summer that would help her not only learn about improving as an administrator but help her identify a network of professionals in similar roles.

YEAR 2

Returning to school in the fall, Ashley felt ready. Her principal was correct. The second year was much better than the first. Student discipline was more controlled through the new Positive Behavior Interventions and Supports system, and it was implemented with fidelity. Kinks and tiny fires still occurred, but Ashley felt much more equipped to deal with student issues, especially those that involved contacting difficult parents and guardians. Year two came with several experiences involving staff conflict, which was an area she had little experience. Working closely with her principal as a coach, she learned how to listen to adults, validate their feelings, defuse tense situations, and work to mediate issues they had among one another.

In February, Ashley's principal told her that he had begun applying for superintendent positions throughout the state. She knew that he was a great leader and that he had been going to school to earn another certification, but this gave her many things to consider when thinking about her own future. In no way did she feel ready to become lead principal, but if she wanted to return to the library, she would have to decide at the end of the school year. She loved her school, students, and community. She also enjoyed being a larger part of the process of helping others and impacting their lives.

In March, Ashley found out she was expecting her second child. Her principal also told her two weeks later that he had accepted a position nearly three hours away as a superintendent of a large school district. These were two secrets she was prepared to keep, one much longer than the other. She prayed and confided in her principal about the weight of the decision. He coached her and reminded her to keep at the center the reason why she originally accepted the position as assistant principal. "Everything happens for a reason," he told her. "I really think that I was brought here to help bring you into this position, you were made to be the principal of this school."

In May, the principal's job was posted, and Ashley applied after receiving support from her work tribe. Within a few weeks, she learned that she had been named principal. The announcement was bittersweet. She knew the next few weeks would be difficult with her transition into becoming the leader at her school and starting the process of finding a new assistant principal. She also still had to tell her new boss that she was in fact a first-year principal who was going to be taking maternity leave in November.

ADJUSTING TO THE ROLE AS PRINCIPAL

Year three was a blur. There were so many new things that happened, and many of them were good. A highly capable and genuine leader was hired as the assistant principal. Ashley and the new assistant had worked together at the school previously as teachers and complemented each other well. They improved school culture and revamped the instructional team process by creating a family-like atmosphere among the faculty and staff. Ashley took maternity leave in November and was back after Christmas break ready to finish the year strong.

Then the COVID-19 pandemic happened. The staff prepared for what they mistakenly thought was a short-term shutdown, as the impact of the virus was unknown. The four days after the shutdown was announced seemed like a whirlwind. Soon, the school launched full-on virtual instruction. Everyone was scared, but Ashley wanted to try to keep all her people together and continue her mission to improve culture.

Ashley, along with the rest of her administrative team, worked together to host Zoom meetings that focused on culture and promoting positive thinking to help those suffering through this time of uncertainty. They had virtual game night, trivia night, and a student talent show. The time was difficult as teachers and students were doing things they had never done before. The lessons Ashley learned during this time were valuable as they kept her focused on serving and taking care of people.

The next school year was consumed by COVID protocols that schools would adhere to during the pandemic. Ashley and her team continued to put students and people first by working to keep the mood light during this strange time. Teacher stress was at an all-time high as faculty were asked to manage both virtual and in-person students simultaneously. The administrative team cleared as many things from teachers' plates as possible by taking over duties and advocating for the halt of irrelevant paperwork.

WHERE SHE WAS NEEDED MOST

Then on a Sunday morning in May, Ashley received a call from one of the district technicians, who was also a parent of a student in her building, as well as her neighbor. She knew before answering the call that something had to be wrong, as it was not even 7:00 a.m.

Upon answering the phone, she found on the other end a very concerned neighbor. "We have a problem," he said. "I was leaving early this morning to run into work, and I have one of your girl students sleeping on my porch." Ashley knew that the sleeping visitor was more than likely a friend of the technician's kid. After explaining to her that the student was laying on the porch wrapped in a blanket, he said that he invited her into his house and immediately called Ashley. He had tried to reach out to the girl's guardian but hadn't received any response.

"Let me throw on some clothes, and I will be right there. We can take her home." Ashley knew some history about this student, whose name was Kate, and knew that the guardian could be difficult to reach. She made a phone call to her mother to come and watch her kids and then quickly grabbed a sweatshirt and a pair of jogging pants.

Upon arriving at the technician's house, Ashley found a very upset young girl. Kate told her she was being sent away to live with someone else, as the current guardian was no longer willing to keep her in their home. Ashley talked with her and calmed her down. She explained to her that running away was not the best decision. She reasoned with the girl that perhaps her guardian would be looking for her and could have even called the police. Finally, Kate agreed to go home.

Ashley, the student, and the technician got into the car and began backing out of the driveway. "Mrs. Westfall?" A small voice from the backseat shyly spoke. "I think I need to go to the hospital."

Ashley's heart dropped, immediate panic and horrible thoughts crossed her mind. "Ok, Kate. Why do we need to go to the hospital?" she asked.

The scared girl replied, "I took a lot of pills before I came here." Ashley and the technician looked at each other.

"How many pills?" Ashley asked.

Kate responded quietly. "I don't really know, maybe 30 or 40."

"We need to go to the hospital," Ashley said to the technician. They drove Kate to the emergency room, while they continued to try to contact her guardian. Multiple calls were made to the superintendent, the guidance counselor, Ashley's assistant principal, child protective services, social workers, and others. Ashley could not leave her student though.

"I am scared, Mrs. Westfall," Kate whispered as she shook with fear.

Ashley held the girl's hand. "It is going to be ok. I am not leaving. I am going to stay right here."

Ashley made a phone call to her mother to let her know that she would not be home in time for church. Her mom was concerned, but Ashley explained that she could no't leave her student and that she was where she needed to be at the moment. "Please pray Mom. I am worried about her and am not sure how I can help."

Ashley did not leave Kate's side. The girl began vomiting and became feverish. Ashley held her and helped clean her up when she was finished. She continued to pray and brought Kate a cold washcloth.

Nurses and doctors were in and out, running tests and starting IVs. The IVs came with tears and panic. "You can do hard things, just take a deep breath," Ashley reminded Kate.

Thankfully, a nurse was able to get the IV started with the first stick. Hours passed and still no one was able to reach the guardian. The police were then sent to the home and finally were able to reach someone. Even after contacting the guardian, it took several hours for anyone to arrive at the hospital.

"I don't know what I have done, Mrs. Westfall. They will never let me go back now." Kate seemed to have no hope, and tears streamed down both of their faces.

"You will be ok, but you cannot ever try to hurt yourself again," Ashley told her student. Kate agreed and promised she would never try to hurt herself again.

Ashley offered comfort. "My students are all like my children to me. When you go through hard things, it hurts my heart."

Kate looked at her. "Why didn't you leave earlier?"

Ashley thought about that question for a moment. "Because this is where I am supposed to be—here with you."

When the guardian finally arrived, Ashley stepped out to speak with him and let the guidance counselor, who had been waiting, come in and talk to Kate. Ashley explained to the guardian what had happened. "I am going to go back in and stay a while longer," Ashley explained. "I need to make sure she is okay before I leave."

"I thought I wasn't going to see you again," Kate said with a sad look in her eye.

Ashley knew that she was going to have to leave soon and allow others to take over. "I will always be here for you, Katie girl. The doctors say that you are going to be ok, but you do have a lot of explaining to do."

Kate looked at her and said, "Is this goodbye?" Teary-eyed, Ashley told her, "No, this is see you soon. I love you, and I know you are going to be okay. Remember the promise you made to me."

Kate nodded her head. "I promise."

When Ashley arrived home, she hugged her own children tightly. Understanding that sometimes being an administrator required you to also be a parent and protector to your students at school was a lesson she had learned today. Kate was discharged right before Ashley left the hospital, and her placement was still being determined by social workers. Ashley was notified that night that the student would not be returning to her school. She was broken.

UNDERSTANDING WHY

As the pandemic became more manageable, things became more normal the following year. Nevertheless, struggles were still present, and being an administrator was still difficult at times. Ashley continued to love her students and staff, but sometimes the pressure of serving them and carrying their burdens as her own was crushing. She still questioned her decision to become an administrator, as she struggled to juggle her many responsibilities at school and her two small children at home.

Extracurricular activities resumed, and as a result, student clubs also started again. Several teachers throughout the building wanted to sponsor a Christian-based club for students, much like the Fellowship of Christian Athletes. Ashley agreed that this was an excellent idea, as it followed her mission to make school a great place for students and staff. The club had a huge response when advertised to students and community.

At the first meeting, students and community members were invited to come and worship together. The gathering was held early in the morning before school. Those who came enjoyed a message from a local pastor and a student-led prayer. Ashley would not miss this service, as she was proud of her students for making the commitment to come to school to pray together. She was overwhelmed with the support she felt from others at this meeting. After the prayer ended, she was on her way to the office and had an epiphany-like moment of realization.

"I now know." Ashley whispered to herself. "I know why I was chosen for this." Silently she prayed and thanked the Lord for showing her that she was in fact in the right place and position. As difficult as the first few years had been and as unsure as she was to lead, she was where she needed to be, and not by chance. Her leadership style was that of a servant and being there for others. Creating an environment that served and loved all students regardless of their background, circumstances, or faith was at the heart of her mission for leading her school.

Understanding that she was meant for leadership changed Ashley. She began to hold closer to her heart the things that made her a unique leader.

For too long she had viewed leaders as excellent public speakers and those who could change the tide by inspiring people with their words. The truth is, leaders come in all forms, and Ashley finally started to see this. She modeled a servant's heart to lead her school and community. For the first time since she had stepped into the role of an administrator, she knew that it was right to lead by being herself and caring for others.

QUESTIONS FOR REFLECTION

- Does being a good leader require certain strengths or attributes?
- What qualities do servant leaders possess?
- Why is coaching important for servant leaders?

FURTHER READING

Covey, S. (2014). *The leader in me: How schools around the world are inspiring greatness, one child at a time.* Simon and Schuster.

Greenleaf, R. (2003). *The Servant-Leader Within.* Paulist Press.

7

Beth's Road to Servant Leadership

Rosemarie Young

> *What we do for ourselves dies with us. What we do for others and the world is and remains immortal.* —Albert Pine

Beth, for as long as she could remember, always wanted to be a teacher. She had a dear aunt who taught for 35 years before retiring—and after retirement, volunteered her time to tutor students. Beth remembered going to her aunt's school to help her set up her classroom for the year. She loved handing new decorations to her aunt as she displayed them throughout the classroom. She was even more excited when she got to go to school one day to visit her and her class. The students respected her aunt and seemed to really love being in her class.

When Beth arrived at the university, she quickly learned where the School of Education was and often walked by the classrooms where she would take her education classes. She was an eager learner and enjoyed all her education classes. The four years flew by, and she graduated and applied for various teaching positions. Imagine Beth's joy when she was selected to teach at her aunt's previous school. Now her aunt was helping *her* to set up *her* classroom.

While assisting Beth in the classroom, her aunt shared her mantra, coined by Teddy Roosevelt, that guided her work as a teacher, "No one cares how much you know, until they know how much you care." Beth took this to heart and worked hard to build relationships with her students, parents, and colleagues. She volunteered for various school committees and every Parent Teacher Association (PTA) activity. She loved the interactions with people, especially when she was able to help with a problem or issue. Beth was respected as a reflective, highly effective educator who was able to build relationships, even with some of the most difficult students and families.

Beth's first master's degree was in the area of teacher leadership. The classes were helpful in developing her collaboration skills and a passion for supporting her colleagues. Her principal supported her growth and encouraged her to continue her leadership journey. Beth soon became a team leader and member of the school advisory committee and loved every challenge this extra service provided.

After a few years, Beth began thinking about going back to school and began to consider what she would study. She admired her principal and often sought her advice on various issues. So, when it came to Beth furthering her education, she knew her principal would be a valued advisor. Beth had looked at various programs and was considering the possibility of becoming a literacy specialist or school counselor. When she met with her principal, she was thrown a curve ball that she has not considered. Her principal encouraged her to consider the principalship as her next goal.

Beth was not sure she could do this and talked with her special aunt. Her aunt encouraged her to consider the principalship program by talking her through all the invaluable work she had done at her school to support students, families, and colleagues. Beth began to think of the impact she could have, and she developed a vision of the type of principal she might become. Finally, she went for it, and the principal preparation program she decided to study under stressed the need for servant leadership in establishing a collaborative and cohesive culture in the schools.

The more Beth learned about servant leadership, the more she realized this was her aunt's passion, and it had now become hers. She especially liked the field activities of the program. Her principal became even more of a mentor and provided numerous learning opportunities for her. Additionally, Beth took on more leadership opportunities and contributed good ideas to various school improvements that everyone appreciated. She was low key in her approach and worked hard to build understanding and support among the staff. Through all of this, she learned some things that would stick with her: Everything is possible with passion, collaboration, teamwork, and the importance of understanding that it was not about self—but about what one could do for the school community in collaboration with community members.

Soon Beth was asked to serve on various district committees. At first, she was hesitant but remembered that the work was not about her but about bettering the school community. Again, she took her servant leadership vision and made strong contributions to every committee she served. Now she had attracted the attention of the district superintendent, who requested Beth to attend a meeting in early January. She thought the superintendent was going to ask her to serve on another committee.

At the meeting, the superintendent threw Beth a curve ball that she was not expecting. She began by sharing some of the feedback she had gotten on

Beth's work at her school and on the district committees. About this time, the principal of her present school walked into the meeting and related that she intended to retire at the end of the current school year. Beth then heard words from the superintendent that both excited her and scared her. She told Beth that she wanted her to consider becoming the principal of the school. The superintendent shared that she had done her homework by talking with advisory council members, teachers and staff, families, community members, and even students—a common theme heard was Beth's focus on servant leadership.

The superintendent noted Beth's selflessness and the benefits of her leadership on the various committees. All of this left Beth speechless, but she was able to mumble, "Wow! I am overwhelmed with this vote of confidence, and I am appreciative of all that you have said. What success I have had has been the collaborative work of so many people. I am honored to work with such outstanding educators and have learned what it takes to run an effective school. My principal has been such a great mentor and saw something in me that I did not see. Again, I am honored and will strongly consider this over the weekend. Thank you!"

Beth's weekend flew by. Of course, she talked to her aunt, went to lunch with her principal, and talked with close colleagues about this possibility. Each person expressed their confidence in Beth's abilities to be an effective school leader. Her aunt shared, "I have observed all that you have done in support of your students and colleagues. You live the mantra that guided my work. Everyone knows you care and that it is not about you but what you can do to support others—a true servant leader. This is what our schools need."

Beth's principal shared, "I have learned so much from you, and I know it is more than you learned from me. You have the credibility, passion, and skills to work with all facets of the school community. People trust you to do what is best for the school, and they know that you care about their well-being while challenging them to improve and stretch. You model what is needed and there is no job or duty that you would not do alongside your staff. I know you are ready, and I pledge to support you any way I can. You can do this!"

After a restless Sunday night of sleep, Beth had made her decision. Early Monday morning, she called the superintendent to share that she would accept the principalship, knowing that she had the support of the community and district. The superintendent stated that she was happy for Beth and the school community. She also shared that she was going to release her from her teaching duties in order to provide transition time for becoming the principal. As Beth ended the call, she took a great sigh and told herself that there was no turning back now.

At the end of the day, the principal called an emergency meeting of all staff. Beth wondered what was going on but didn't have time to think about it with the business of the teaching day. One of Beth's team members asked if she could talk with her about an issue with a student. Beth reminded her that they had a faculty meeting after school, so she could not talk much but would be willing to talk more after the meeting if needed. Later, Beth realized that her colleague really did not need her advice. The colleague's devious plan was to slow down Beth's arrival to the faculty meeting.

As Beth walked into the faculty meeting, she noticed the balloons and treats. Next, she noticed a banner that said, "Congratulations, Principal Beth! We will follow you anywhere!" Beth gave her team member the *eye* and walked into the room. One person after another spoke to the amazing qualities of Beth and how excited they were to continue working with her. Central to all comments was her special way of putting people first and truly being a servant.

When it came time for Beth to speak, she took a breath and shared her journey to leadership: the influence of her aunt and her love of teaching; the amazing people she worked with; and the honor of being selected as the next principal. She pledged to work hard every day to champion the well-being of the school community. She sincerely thanked everyone for their support and allowing her to serve as their next principal. That afternoon Beth knew she had made the right decision and pledged to be the leader the school deserved.

As the years went by, Beth remained true to her pledge. She consistently worked with her teachers to provide them with what they needed to be effective. Beth would remind them that she trusted their judgment and would find a way to obtain what they needed. One example was when the school was implementing a new math program and there were not funds available to purchase supplementary manipulatives. Beth worked with the district and community to open an after-school math lab for families and found high school students who would tutor students after school. Community businesses provided the funds to purchase the materials.

Another example was the need for classroom sets of books to be used during literacy time. Again, Beth reached out to her community and families to support this need. In return, the books were put in baggies with a sticker letting the community know who had provided the funds for the project. And, when a teacher expressed an interest to know about Science, Technology, Art, Math (STEAM) education, Beth worked with a local university to provide a workshop on it.

Community members knew that Beth was there to support them, too. Beth would recognize supportive community agencies and businesses at PTA meetings and Family Nights while encouraging the families to support them through patronage. Beth spearheaded numerous collections for families when a parent lost a job or when a tragedy struck the community. In each instance, the emphasis was to acknowledge those who had contributed and not the role she played. When asked why she never took credit, she would say, "Nothing can be done without the support of our community members. I just serve to have our school as the collection site. The community really does the work."

Beth was loved by her staff and community, and she truly loved each of them. Very seldom did she make a request that was not fulfilled. Staff and community members would relate the numerous times she came through for them, so how could they not be supportive of her?

When retirement came, Beth had such mixed feelings, but realized that the school was in a great place and the vision of an unselfish school culture would continue. People understood the value of this type of leadership and the significant school accomplishments that resulted from it.

Beth's retirement party was huge—with teachers, staff members, students, families, community, board members, and district administrators all in attendance. One testimonial after another shared the difference she has made and provided numerous examples of her caring leadership. The celebration ended with the school's library being named after her.

Beth, of course, was overwhelmed with the crowd and memories. She never thought any of what she did was that special. It was what she thought a good leader should do, as it was not about the leader but what the leader could do for others, as well as developing the capacity of others.

Beth summed it up at the end of the recognition: "I have been humbled by the outpouring today. My aunt, whom I loved dearly, taught me that educators must care for others and build strong relationships. In building these strong relationships, you come to know the heart and soul of people. And once this happens, you are bound to do whatever you can to keep that heart and soul strong it is what every school community needs and those who are fortunate enough to become a school leader, must keep the flame of hope and promise strong. In the end, I received so much more because of your hearts and souls. Thank you for this special day and remember that I love each of you. Do you think I could come back and volunteer from time to time?"

QUESTIONS FOR REFLECTION

- In what ways have you served as a servant leader in your school or community?
- What are the benefits to schools and communities of a servant leader in the school leader's role?
- What examples of servant leadership have you observed, and what examples of missed opportunities can you identify?

FURTHER READING

Brown, Brené. (2018). *Dare to Lead: Brave Work, Tough Conversations, Whole Heart*. New York: Random House.
Roosevelt, T. Quote: Nobody cares how much you know, until . . . brainyquote.com

8

What Do You Need from Me?

(Especially Considering I Am Only Here Approximately Half of the Time?)

Lewis Willian

> *Servant leadership is to "empower the people you lead to grow personally and professionally."*—Unknown

Jake was excited to start his first principal's position. After a decade as a high school chemistry teacher, he had decided that he needed to be an elementary principal. He wanted to have formative impact on the development of children before they settled into a routine of bad habits as a teenager. He saw many teens come through his high school classes that he was certain had needed a positive role model earlier in their life. He wanted to be that role model and have influence earlier in their development.

Therefore, with his elementary principal's degree, he started applying for administrative openings to work with younger students. The first job he was offered was to serve as the principal of two small elementary schools at the same time. Situated in the foothills of the Appalachian Mountains, these schools were only eight miles apart—but separated by twisting roads and valleys that prohibited safe transport of students between them. Therefore, the district allowed these two small schools to stay open. It was not the most cost-effective way to organize a school district, but it did allow for students to have community schools where families were highly involved in their school.

At first, Jake tried to follow the same schedule that his retired predecessor had kept: One day on one campus and then the next day on the other campus. This took Jake back and forth between buildings every other day. He soon found that this schedule did not work for him. It seemed that he always needed to be at the "other" school. As soon as he arrived at one building, the phone would ring, and the other school would have some crisis that needed to be fixed. He found he needed to be at both places every day. So, he adjusted his schedule to do a half day one building—drive the eight miles and do a half day at the other building, and then switched out the next day.

At first, that arrangement seemed to work better. With a presence in each building each day, Jake could handle issues in a timely manner. However, he started noticing a pattern of teachers rushing to him with problems as soon as he arrived at midday. Teachers would stand at the door during lunch, waiting for his car to pull up outside—expecting him to immediately work on their specific problem as soon as his feet entered the building. Cleaning up the messes and "putting out brush fires" consumed his afternoons on a regular basis. Vision casting and culture work had to be put on the back shelf. Immediate managerial concerns took precedent over long-term people and relationship concerns. A few months in, Jake began to wonder how he could change the schools' cultures to remedy these daily occurrences.

Jake had been taught in his principal preparation program that a good first step for a new principal was to schedule one-hour "listening" sessions with each staff member. These sessions were more than a meet-and-greet conversation—they were important to initially hear concerns and to share his vision for the school. Toward the end of each of these conferences, Jake pointedly asked the same questions each time.

These questions generated a myriad of responses, even categories of responses. Some of the teachers had an immediate list of concerns, most of them in response to how the last principal had led the buildings. Jake could see that some issues had roots with the previous administration. Some teachers did not like how the building had been managed under Jake's predecessor. They wanted change, and they wanted it immediately.

In these conversations, Jake could hear remnants of years of frustrated and unfulfilled teachers. A common theme was that they wanted firm behavioral expectations that allowed them to teach without interruption. Any misbehaving student that was sent to the office was to be dealt with swiftly and definitively. In short, these teachers wanted a firmer hand from the principal.

And other teachers reflected a bit longer before they spoke. Their responses varied from "I just want you to listen to me when I need to talk," to "I want to feel supported when I have to correct the students and the parents don't like it."

The most common response from teachers was that they needed an administrator who would listen to them and value their opinions when making decisions. This did not mean that the teachers expected to always get "their" way. Instead, they wanted to feel that their input was valued and considered when the principal and council had to make choices. They wanted to feel empowered in their school. They wanted to feel like they had ownership of their professional career.

Sometimes the principal would have to make a different decision than what the teachers preferred. But, if they felt like they had participated in an open and honest dialogue about the reasons the decision was made, they could usually go along with their honest and open administrator. When teachers feel like they are not heard on any issue, they become resentful and withdrawn. Therefore, the best way to serve your teachers is to engage them.

At the end of Jake's series of conferences, he posted a summary of what the teachers asked for on the projector screen at the beginning of a faculty meeting. Without including specifics that would become personally identifiable, he posted a bulleted list of everyone's responses to his questions for the entire faculty to review. He then allowed the teachers to have an open and honest discussion to narrow that list down to the key things they all needed from their principal.

As that discussion unfolded, some of the smaller individual selfish items began to vanish off the list and major group needs rose to the top. Issues like the need to be heard surfaced. At the end of the discussion, a new understanding was forged between administration and teachers regarding the expectations for both. Many of the expectations became broader, vision-setting, building-level implementation work focused on systems rather than specific concerns such as, "You need to talk to Johnny's parents because he's misbehaving."

In order to free the principal to do the agreed upon work, the teachers began to own their students' discipline problems under a building-wide systematic approach to constructive behavior. In other words, the principal begins to be a leader and not a manager.

Fast-forward five years into Jake's tenure as the principal. Teachers no longer met him at the door when he transferred between schools with "brush fires to put out." Jake was able to enter the building and work on initiatives that needed to be addressed and implemented, increasing the faculty's productivity many times over. He did institute a process of walking through the building as soon as he arrived, stopping by the door of every classroom to see the students and make eye contact with the teachers. Generally, a smile and a nod was enough to let him know everything was working well that day.

If there was an issue that a teacher could not handle in the classroom, the teacher would wave Jake over and make an appointment to see him. Empowerment for teachers to address issues in their own classroom led to a far greater learning experience for students and a far more productive school.

A good definition of servant leadership is to "empower the people you lead to grow personally and professionally." Jake found that if you just take time to listen you can lead more effectively, because you know the needs of your people. It was not necessary to bow to the individual will of individual staff members, but it was necessary to listen.

QUESTIONS FOR REFLECTION

- What are the questions you would ask your staff right now?
- What other methods would you have of finding the "pulse"/current status in your building?
- Why is it important for the administrator to focus on the big issues in the building?

FURTHER READING

Grisson, J., Egalite, A., Lindsay, C. (2019). *How principals affect students and schools: A systematic synthesis of two decades of research.* Wallace Foundation. https://www.wallacefoundation.org/knowledge-center

Wall, P. (2016). One principal, two schools. *The Atlantic.* https://www.theatlantic.com/education/archive/2016/08

9

COVID-19

Tabetha Housekeeper

I've learned that people will forget what you said, people will forget what you did, but people will never forget how you made them feel.— Maya Angelou

The sun was shining, and children were buzzing around the playground of Maple Elementary School. It was the second week of March and everyone within the Maple community was starting to get spring fever. Although winter had decided to linger a bit longer than the year before, March seemed to bring about hope for new beginnings. The members of the Maple community had spent the previous six months hearing of a terrible virus that was quickly spreading throughout the world. Newspaper articles, social media posts, news channels, and local health officials shared daily safety alerts to warn everyone of the inevitable spread of the dangerous virus. Kelly, the principal of Maple Elementary, knew she had to begin preparing her students and staff for hard times that everyone could feel approaching.

Kelly had only been a principal for about eighteen months when COVID-19 hit the Maple community. She had been a teacher for ten years and had taught at Maple Elementary for five years when she decided to walk through the doors of school administration. Being "the boss" had never been a desire of Kelly's; however, she believed in the people of Maple Elementary and knew that she did not want to see someone else lead the school who may not care for the staff and students the way she did. So, when the opportunity to be principal of Maple Elementary opened, she agreed to take on the challenge. Within the first year of being a principal, Kelly learned many difficult lessons, but none of those lessons would compare to the challenging ones she was about to learn in her second year.

It was a normal Tuesday morning at Maple Elementary. Buses were right on schedule; the car line was running smoothly; kids were flooding into the school building; and teachers were greeting students with smiles and high-fives. Kelly was taking her normal stroll through the school to check with staff and say, "Good morning" to students. Around 7:30 a.m., Kelly's phone rang, and it was a principal from another elementary school.

"Are your teachers freaking out about the possibility of shutting down school?" Linda, the other principal asked.

"When? What do you mean?" Kelly replied.

"This morning. Apparently, there was something posted on social media yesterday evening that is making my teachers and staff think we are shutting down after today," Linda shared.

Kelly had not heard the possibility of schools shutting down in her community but had read articles of other school districts in the country having to close their doors due to the spread of COVID-19. "Goodness! I sure hope we are not shutting down. What will students do if their parents are working all day?" Kelly was beginning to worry.

"Or what about our staff? We only have two weeks until spring break. I wonder how long we will have to be out." Linda was convinced that the rumor she heard was true.

Unfortunately, the worries of Linda's staff did come true. Only two days later, lead principals were pulled together by the district superintendent, and he shared that all schools in the Maple community would close their doors.

"During these two weeks prior to spring break, I want all of you to ensure that there are no staff members in the building. We must practice quarantining away from each other in order to keep the spread of the virus at bay. Staff members need to be reminded and encouraged to stay at home as much as possible. Our local health department has asked me to close the doors of our facilities. That means everyone needs to stay home."

Kelly walked out of that meeting with the superintendent and other principals with the color drained from her face, as she felt the tension in her neck and chest. She could see flashes of her students' faces. Her worry began to grow exponentially as she thought about specific students and their stories. One family had three children that attended Maple Elementary who had just lost their father. It had only been two months since his passing, and the three children were finally able to attend school without crying for their mother.

"What will they do all day at home? Who will watch them on days that their mother has to work? What about the students who are being abused, and now they are going to have to stay home with the person who has been hurting them? What will happen to the eighteen students who are being raised by grandparents? How will their grandparents stay safe from COVID-19? How will students get food if a family does not have means for transportation?

Who will supervise the younger students?" Kelly could not stop the fears and worries from speeding through her brain as she drove back to Maple Elementary.

There was a district-wide announcement made via email to all staff members on Thursday afternoon, explaining the imminent need for schools to close their doors for at least two weeks. School was dismissed at 2:35 p.m. Kelly went outside and directed traffic like it was a normal day. She walked back into the school at 3:05 p.m. on the dot. Upon entering the building, she heard a roar of chatter. She looked up to see the entire staff of Maple Elementary standing in the library. The look of fear, worry, and anxiety were all over their faces. The news had come hard and fast that school would be shutting down and Kelly had not had a minute to think about addressing the news with her staff. She knew there would be many questions she could not answer, but she had expected more time to prepare.

Every other big change that Kelly had experienced since being a principal came with time to process, time to collaborate with other principals, and time to get guidance from central office staff who were more equipped and experienced than her. This bomb was dropped on everyone, and no one was prepared for it. Kelly walked toward the crowd in the library and said a quick prayer in her head, "Lord you know their needs, fears, and worries. Help me to calm rather than make it worse."

As she approached the group, Kelly felt numb and her face was tingling with stress. As she entered the library, the crowd of teachers, custodians, and other staff grew quiet and turned to face her. In this moment, she remembered something that a mentor had told her early within her first year as principal, "One thing you can never forget about leadership is that it is lonely at the top, but everyone will use you as a barometer to gauge how to respond in critical situations."

"Be the barometer," Kelly thought as she looked around at the faces in the library and waited for a few other staff members to trickle in. She stood in the middle of the room pondering her next move. All she could think about was how this situation was never taught in school. As far as she knew, there were no books written about strategies to use when dealing with a world pandemic. Kelly took a long deep breath and finally spoke to her staff.

"Well guys. It is time to think with our hearts. At the beginning of this school year we all agreed that our *North Star*, the thing we would focus on this entire school year, would be relationships. We have spent months working on building positive, meaningful relationships with each other and teaching our students how to build healthy relationships with others in their lives. What if we had not created that *North Star* focus?" She took a long pause to let her staff digest and reflect for a few seconds. "I can't help but to believe that our relationships with each other and your ability to love your students are the very things that will get us through this hard time."

Kelly spoke from the heart. "I know you are scared. All of us are scared for our students, our own families, and for our own health. I also know that you have thousands of questions for me regarding what your life will look like until after spring break. I may be able to answer some of those questions but not all at this time. So, later tonight I will send you a form so that you can fill it with all your fears, worries, concerns, and questions. Right now, I have three things I want you to do for this evening."

"First, I want you to take some time to think about tomorrow. Our students are coming to school for one more day and then they will be home for at least three weeks. What can we do to make sure they feel safe and leave here feeling loved tomorrow? Secondly, think about what you do best. How can you use your greatest strengths to continue the outpouring of love to our Maple Elementary family during this unprecedented time? And the last thing I want you to do tonight is, spend time with the ones you love most."

Kelly looked around the room and saw blank stares mixed with tears. She was not sure how to end this conversation when she knew that some of her people expected immediate answers. There were staff members who would be relieved by her three requests, but she could feel the frustrations and disappointments from a handful who wanted more explanation and more guidance. The truth of the situation was that Kelly did not have any more information. In fact, no one had more information or guidance on how to be prepared. Before Kelly dismissed the staff, she decided to do one more thing before everyone walked away.

"Guys, I have only one tool in my toolbox to help us through the next few weeks, months, and maybe even years. Will you pray with me?" Kelly held her hands out and reached for a staff member on each side of her. Slowly, others started to reach for a hand until finally, everyone was holding hands with someone on each side. There was a large circle joined together in the middle of the library. Kelly prayed with transparency and asked for peace to fill the hearts of her staff. After the prayer, some staff members stood around and continued their conversations. Other staff members quickly left the room to begin preparing for the next day.

Kelly walked back to her office, shut the door, and cried. She felt like a bad leader. She had always tried to be prepared and practice clear communication to her staff. However, she was worried that everything she had just said was an epic fail. She had no idea how to help ease their minds during this terrible time. Kelly did communicate with other principals that evening, but none of them knew how to handle this situation either. Just like when she was teaching in the classroom, she knew that it would be impossible to make decisions about her school based on how other principals were dealing with their own schools; however, she was hoping to steal some good ideas at least. There were none to steal.

Kelly spent Thursday evening doing exactly what she had asked her staff to do. She thought about the Maya Angelou quote, "People will forget what you said, people will forget what you did, but people will never forget how you made them feel." Kelly knew that her staff needed to feel supported, but more than that they needed to feel free to think with their hearts. She spent the evening with her family, and they discussed their own worries and fears about the upcoming change.

"How will we get groceries? How long will we be out of school? We can't even play our sports. Why can't we leave our house to go to a friend's house? What do you mean we can't go anywhere?" Kelly's children had their own questions.

The alarm clock sounded at 5:15 a.m., which was Kelly's normal time to wake up. She did not feel ready for the day. She knew that by this time, the shutdown had been communicated with families. She felt even less prepared to discuss details of this decision with families than she did with staff. Again, she used the only tool she had for this unsettling situation. She prayed for God to help her make her staff feel supported and loved so that they could have the freedom to do what was in their hearts.

Friday was truly a blur. Parents were calling and flooding the front office by 7:15 a.m., asking if students were bringing home computers, homework, books, etc. Kelly and her office staff shared the same message repeatedly.

"Make sure you have a working email on file in our system. Your child's teacher will be reaching out next week with more information," was repeated all day long. As Kelly circulated throughout the school that day, she saw teachers encouraging their students to fill their backpacks with books from the teachers' personal classroom libraries. She saw teachers making plastic baggies filled with pencils, crayons, markers, flashcards, drawing paper, and even snacks for students to take home.

Other teachers wrote personalized notes to students and then placed them in their backpacks, while others had their doors decorated with streamers and balloons to welcome students back to school. The librarian was encouraging students to check out more than one book at a time, even though her policy had been only one book per student prior. Students were leaving the library with more books in their hands than usual, bookmarks, and some even had books for their parents to read.

During lunch, Kelly entered the cafeteria to see if everything was okay. She glanced down at one student's tray and saw a banana with a smiley face drawn on it with a marker. She thought maybe the student had snuck a marker into the cafeteria until she started noticing that every student in the cafeteria had smiley faces drawn on their fruit.

Kelly went into the kitchen area and she heard music playing. There were three cafeteria staff and the cafeteria manager dancing to "Don't Worry, Be Happy," while they were serving a group of 2nd grade lunches. Oranges and bananas that were being served had happy faces on them. Then at the end of the line, the custodian was handing out extra chips, granola bars, and snacks that students could take home with them if they wanted. Kids were smiling as they exited the cafeteria line.

Kelly just shook her head in disbelief as she exited the cafeteria. The same staff she saw with fear and dread on their faces the day before had decided to create an atmosphere of joy in Maple Elementary. Kelly had expected that Friday to be drab and filled with sadness or worry because that is exactly how she felt inside. Despite having to answer questions from scared parents and families, that Friday had been a day filled with hope. As Kelly rounded the corner to her office, she was stopped by the music teacher, who was never one to want to "go off cuff." She liked order, structure, and had high expectations for her students.

"Hey Kelly. I have an idea. Do you have a minute?" The music teacher asked.

"Sure." Kelly replied.

"Would it be okay for me to play some music over the intercom while the students are dismissing to the buses? I just think it would send them off on a good note."

Kelly could not believe she had not thought of this idea. "I would love that. Thank you so much for thinking of it."

Around 2:10 p.m. Kelly was standing in the hallway getting ready for dismissal when the guidance counselor of Maple Elementary came over the school intercom.

"Good afternoon Maple Elementary family. This is Mrs. Rodgers. I just wanted to let all of you know that the next few weeks may feel different. The days may even be hard at times but, boys and girls, I want to remind you that all of you have the tools you need to do hard things. Your teachers, your principal, and all the adults at Maple Elementary love you so much. Be strong, be kind, and remember that you have everything you need inside of you to overcome anything. Have an amazing long spring break!"

About that time, "Celebration," by Kool and the Gang, came blaring through the school intercom. Kindergarten teachers led their students down the hallway and toward the bus lot, dancing and waving their arms in the air. Most students were laughing or smiling while they struggled to carry loads of books, binders, snacks, and other supplies home with them. Each grade filed out dancing, waving, and giving hugs to teachers and staff as they headed toward the bus. The car line was bouncing with energetic students and teachers giving hugs as they transitioned students to their parents. The custodians had even stopped their afternoon chores to come outside and wave "goodbye" to the busses and to the cars as they left Maple Elementary School for what everyone thought would be three weeks.

Kelly stood on the sidewalk of Maple Elementary on that chilly but sunny Friday. She waved "goodbye" to her students as they were dismissed. She took a deep breath and thought, "Lord please go with them." As she turned to go back into the school, she lifted her head to see a wall in front of her. This wall was made up of the Maple Elementary staff. Every adult was standing behind her waving, smiling, and shouting, "I love you" to students on the buses. Kelly looked up and said, "Thank you."

The two weeks of closure due to COVID-19, plus the one week of spring break gave everyone a nice break, but Kelly knew the time away from school might be longer. The three weeks turned into six weeks. Then the six weeks turned into the rest of the school year. Before anyone realized it, students had been sent home on March 13, 2020, and had not returned to school in person until late September. COVID raged throughout the entire nation. Businesses were shutting down, churches closed, groceries were becoming more and more scarce, all sporting events had been cancelled, hospitals were struggling to keep staff, and everyone was fearful that someone in their family would be the next victim.

Life was hard for everyone in the Maple community, but the joy and hope spread by the staff of Maple Elementary on March 13th was just the beginning. Kelly and her staff spent countless hours writing positive notes, dropping candy and treats into students' mailboxes, delivering lunches to homes, doing drive-by celebrations for student birthdays, or simply making phone calls to check on families.

Kelly learned a lot during her second year of being a principal, but the most important lesson was that a principal does not always have to know the answers. Leaders need the confidence to step back and give permission and freedom to their followers to do what is in their hearts. Leaders should never forget, "People will forget what you said, people will forget what you did, but people will never forget how you made them feel," Maya Angelou.

QUESTIONS FOR REFLECTION

- How was Kelly an example of servant leadership?
- Why is it important for leaders to give their followers permission to follow their hearts or instinct?
- Do you think leaders should have all the answers? Why or why not?

FURTHER READING

Burkhauser, S., Gates, S., Hamilton, L., & Igemoto, G. (2012). *Challenges and Opportunities Facing Principals in the First Year at a School*. Rand Corporation Research.

McElrath, K. (2020). *Schooling During the COVID 19 Pandemic*. https://www.census.gov/library/stories.html

10

Going and Driving the Extra Mile

Stephanie Sullivan

The servant leader is servant first. It begins with the natural feeling that one wants to serve.—Robert K. Greenleaf

Jane, a native of Graves County, Kentucky, first thought she wanted to be a child psychologist. She loved teaching children and watching them learn; so she transitioned to elementary education. Once she began teaching, she wondered what she could do to make an even greater impact to reach more people. That desire is what led her into an administrative role.

Now an elementary school principal, Jane still sometimes feels like she is a child psychologist, and sometimes even a family therapist. For her, the drive to pursue leadership was because of the impact that could be made on others. It is not just about the positive impact on academics, but it is the desire to see children and families become good citizens and do things they never thought possible, because someone believes in them. Her goal is to help eliminate barriers to help her students be successful.

What does servant leadership mean to you? When Jane responded, she stated that it is being willing to take on a task that you would ask of someone else but doing it with them or in their place . . . Simply put, it is the right thing to do.

How often do educators take on that mindset and go the extra mile? Educators are called to serve those with whom they work, including students, families, and staff. Daily, our schools are filled with those who have dedicated their lives to serving others. Jane's story is just one of many stories that make the role of a leader so important . . . and so special.

DRIVING A BUS

Before COVID and teacher shortages, Jane saw a need and accepted the challenge. Funds were low, and field trips often required students to pay their own transportation costs. Being in a high-poverty school district created an even greater challenge. Believing in the importance of students receiving real-life learning experiences through field trips, Jane decided she would get her Commercial Driver's License (CDL) and drive her own students to their outings away from school, eliminating that expense. She said that it was necessary to get the students to those places that would impact their learning, so she literally began going (or driving) the extra mile. With the money saved on transportation, her students were able to go to more field trips than ever before.

When Jane inquired with the director of transportation about pursuing her CDL license, he supported those efforts, but informed her that he may need her to drive other routes occasionally. So, she had served in that capacity a few times, but when COVID hit, so did a bus driver shortage. Jane eventually accepted a bus route. She felt she had to play a role to get the students to school so they could be educated. If there were no other drivers available, then she would do what was needed. Once again, she was willing to go the extra mile, because "that's just what you do."

During the first year of COVID (2020–21), Jane declined pay for those extra services. She felt that all areas of the schools had been impacted and that it was her responsibility to step in and do what she could to help. She stated, "It's just what you do to keep things going."

As the effects of COVID have started to diminish, Jane no longer drives a regular route, but she still subs two to three days per week as needed. She still does not want to receive pay, but the superintendent has insisted. Jane believes, "Our rewards will come in Heaven."

While taking on leadership in the driver's seat of a bus, Jane has learned a lot about the life of a bus driver. It's hard work. Subbing in the dark on routes you have never driven before can be a daunting task. She believes people have taken for granted how difficult that job is, not to mention having a load of children that may or may not sit in a seat and do what is asked of them. She says, "It is exhausting to do that and then also work all day." But her philosophy is "No one ever said going the extra mile was easy, but it can also be highly rewarding."

Jane has reaped rewards by making positive connections with students. She sometimes drives high school routes after finishing her elementary routes. She stated that the students are no different, regardless of their age. She recommends to just be nice to them, then they will talk to you and do what is expected. She also realizes what a difference the first face they see in the morning can make. Developing those positive relationships both at the beginning and end of the school day can leave a lasting impact on those students.

Jane has learned a lot about people. She related that sadly, parents are amazed that anyone will do things beyond the role of their job description for others, because it is not the world we live in anymore. She claimed that it has been good as an administrator to have shown parents and the community that no one is above anything. Everyone must pitch in and do whatever is needed.

Servant leadership is an important aspect of the principalship. As Jane stated, "If you exhibit servanthood in your own life/profession, when you ask people to go above and beyond, they are willing because you have been an example." She believes that others, when servant leadership has been modeled, will not feel burdened but will be gratified to serve in that way.

BEING THE BRIDGE

Beyond taking on a bus route, Jane has realized the importance of students being in school so they can learn. The parents of her elementary students have learned that if they are unable to get their child to school, Jane will. When a parent calls and says they do not have a car, Jane tells them she is on her way to get them. If parents call and say they got up late and are not going to be at school, Jane says "No, get them ready. I'll come get them." If a child has been absent for a day and no one answers the school's phone call, Jane gets in her car and goes to the house to check on them. She says, "If they are not here, we cannot teach them or feed them." There is little wonder why their school attendance rate is so high!

With COVID, another set of challenges surfaced that impacted learning—and Jane intervened. If parents were unable to go to the school to get their child's schoolwork, then Jane would take it to them. If students were not participating with the virtual instruction, she called the parents. If the students did not have a working computer, she would take one to their home. She claims, "You don't have to do those things long, because they learn that we are going to be at their house."

Jane says this extra effort sets the tone for how important school is. The students don't know why, but they realize this must really be important. This persistence of going the extra mile for student learning is a real-life example of the district's mission put into action . . . Striving for Excellence: No exceptions, no excuses.

YET ANOTHER CRISIS

Beyond the challenges that the pandemic brought to districts across the country, Graves County residents were faced with a disaster on December 10, 2021. The longest and strongest tornado on history tore through Mayfield, Kentucky (Bunting, B. December 17, 2021), which left many families without homes, power, food, and clothes. The following morning, Jane arrived at school to speak with the emergency management personnel. She called the superintendent to tell him that her school had power and showers were available for families, as well as food to feed them. She sent a message to her staff and within an hour, cafeteria staff and others came to the school, bringing food and other supplies.

A video message was sent to the community stating that if families could not get to the school, then the staff would come to them. Many in the community donated toiletries for those in need. Everyone in the building was ready to serve. The school served in this capacity throughout the week until other shelters in the community were secured. Jane added that no one was "on the clock," but that the staff served simply because there was a need.

So, how did Jane develop this heart to be a servant leader? Both her mom and grandmother have been examples for her throughout her life. Growing up in the church, she always heard stories about serving others as self. Being embedded in that environment, she had many models and just naturally adapted to that type of serving because it was what was always lived out in front of her. She also feels that it is what she has been called to do—"a gift that God gave me to serve and lead in that way. My prayer is always to be the brightest light and greatest impact. He opens those doors." She says that when you love people unconditionally, it amazes them, and it also gives them hope. She exemplifies her belief that we do not have to teach it, but live it, for others to know they are loved.

One text that left an impression on Jane during her college years was Carnegie's book, *How to Win Friends and Influence People*. Although a focus of the book is about one's personality, Jane feels that serving others is also an important aspect. As related to the book, some strategies for how to deal with others include providing sincere appreciation and motivating them with the desire to serve.

QUESTIONS FOR REFLECTION

- What are ways administrators can identify areas in which they can provide service to school and community?

- What are ways that sincere appreciation can be shown to student, staff, and/or community?
- How do administrators model and create the desire to serve others among their staff?

FURTHER READING

Bunting, B. (December 17, 2021). Climate Adaptation Center. https://www.theclimateadaptationcenter.org

Carnegie, D. (1936). *How to Win Friends and Influence People*. Simon and Schuster.

11

Gideon's Story

J.P. Rader

Behind every great achievement is a dreamer of great dreams. Much more than a dreamer is required to bring it to reality; but the dream must be there first.—Robert K. Greenleaf

What is servant leadership? Why has it been included in so many leadership biographies in recent years? It is revered but is elusive. It is desirable but also uncomfortable. Robert Greenleaf described the servant leader as the "care taken by the servant—first to make sure that other people's needs are being served." Greenleaf goes on to say that the best test of this is to watch to see if "those served grow as persons; do they, while being served, become healthier, wiser, freer, more autonomous, more likely themselves to become servants." The Bain Inspirational Leadership Model expands on that by saying that servanthood should be about "investing on behalf of others and finding joy in their success."

International schools have, in recent years, embraced the notion of servant leadership as a core element of what inspirational leadership should look like. There are numerous stories of headmasters pouring into the lives of their administration team, principals and assistant principals developing their teachers, and teachers transforming their students all through the lens of servant leadership. Servanthood develops a servant mindset that then develops capacity in the individual. This process is not linear. There are many bumps in the road that cause those involved to back up, reassess, grow, and develop.

The following story illustrates this process and demonstrates what Greenleaf understood . . . Servant leadership is about willingness—willingness to be present, to love unconditionally, to be relational and to serve in a way that moves beyond the boundaries of one job and into another. It demonstrates that belief in a person can propel one forward to a life of service.

GIDEON'S STORY

Gideon was his name. He came from Israel and enrolled at a prestigious international school in Seoul as a rising 10th grade student. His father had been transferred to Korea as a military attaché in the Israeli Embassy. He had a long career in the military as a helicopter pilot and this was his final stop. Gideon's mother was a "stay at home" mom as she was raising four children, the oldest of whom was Gideon.

Gideon was not overly pleased to be transferring to Korea. He saw himself first and foremost as a basketball player, and this move only appeared to make his path more difficult for what he hoped would be a career in basketball. He was not very interested in school, knew no one in Korea, and worst of all, spoke very little English since Hebrew was his first language. He had grown up near Tel Aviv, attending a local school, so this was his first international school experience.

His first day at his new school, Gideon was taken to the high school counselor's office so he could determine his schedule. There he met someone who, at first glance, did not appear to be a person who would change his life, but she did. Her name was Ashley Banterman. Ashley asked Gideon a few questions about what he liked to do, what his interests were, and the subjects he enjoyed in school. The conversation was a bit one-sided. There was some terror on Gideon's part as he realized how limited his vocabulary was. He managed "Hi, my name is Gideon," as well as a few other things that helped her understand that he loved basketball.

Gideon was not pleased. He was a confident person, but this whole international school situation was unnerving. His next stop turned into a much more pleasant encounter, as Ashley took him downstairs to see the secondary principal, her husband, Craig Banterman. Craig had coached the high school boys' basketball team for twenty years, in addition to his duties as an administrator, and was delighted to meet him. The conversation was short as Gideon managed a few sentences. The most important thing he caught was "come out and join us for Monday night basketball." He did not know it but the Bantermans had started him down a path of servant leadership that he could not have foreseen, as they saw something in him he could not completely see in himself.

The Monday night scrimmage led to other introductions and served as a gateway for Gideon into the school. (Isn't that the way it works in so many cases? Sports can be a lifeline.) Gideon's outlook immediately improved and he meshed quickly into school along with his brothers and sister. He cared little for his classes, but Ashley continued to meet with Gideon on a weekly basis, checking in and listening to him. In the meantime, Gideon immediately became involved with the basketball players and started making friends, which led to his English improving.

This particular international school in Seoul is a high-powered school that offers an International Baccalaureate program. It is difficult for English first language speakers, much less someone in Gideon's situation. Nevertheless, he persisted and by the basketball season was conversant and meshing well. Coach Banterman recognized he could play and gave him an immediate opportunity to step into the line-up despite the fact that the team was loaded with excellent players. This was empowering for Gideon; it gave him confidence and led to immediate success. Although the season ended with only three losses, two of them were in championship games, which left a bit of a bitter taste.

As the school year ended, Craig Banterman made a shocking announcement that he was leaving the school after twenty years of administrating, teaching, and coaching in Korea. He had gotten an opportunity to teach and coach at a small Midwestern university. This was hard on Gideon, as he had become very close to his principal and counselor through the various check points. The thought of losing two key mentors was devastating. Surprisingly, the Bantermans announced that Ashley would stay one more year in Seoul to help transition the school in bringing in a new principal before returning to the U.S. Gideon was sad about Mr. Banterman but thrilled that he would continue to have an advocate in Mrs. Banterman who was remaining at the school.

Gideon's English was improving rapidly, and he spent a good bit of time in Mrs. Banterman's office trying to make a plan for the future. Basketball season turned out to be the highlight of the year as he led the team to the two championship titles that had eluded them the previous season. After the season was over, Gideon made a decision that changed his life. He went into Mrs. Banterman's office and asked her if he could go to the U.S. and live with the Bantermans for his senior year and attend school and play basketball in the U.S. Her response was "Gideon, I will talk with Mr. Banterman, and we will make a decision together." She came back a week later and said that they felt called to have him come live with them.

This uncommon act of kindness was Gideon's first encounter with what servant leadership looked like. Sometimes the boundaries of our commitment to servant leadership are extended beyond the job at hand. Gideon's parents were surprisingly in favor of this opportunity and said they would financially support it. Gideon would be forever thankful for their willingness to let him go.

Coming to America

Gideon arrived in Kentucky for his first look at the U.S. The Bantermans immediately went about trying to enroll him in the public county school. The public school administration said he could enroll but could not play basketball due to potential recruiting violations. This was devastating to Gideon. The Bantermans would not let it go and found another opportunity at a local private religious school. That led to a legal battle that finally ended in a hearing with the Kentucky High School Athletic Association, which ruled that Gideon could play during the season because they determined that he had not been recruited. In fact, when Gideon walked into school it was the first time he had ever met the coach.

So, Gideon was able to fulfill his dream of playing high school basketball in the U.S. Unfortunately, the coach had very little interest in integrating new blood into a team that was loaded with seniors. It was a time of soul searching for Gideon. There were many talks with Mr. and Mrs. Banterman, who Gideon now took to calling Mom and Dad, about his frustrations. They supported Gideon, commiserated with him, supported him and kept telling him he had a bright future in basketball. The Banterman's believed in him when he did not believe in himself. This was something that Gideon later learned was a key component of servant leadership the Bantermans demonstrated daily.

Gideon kept working hard, hired a basketball trainer, and improved his game despite the situation. In the meantime, he was accepted into the Banterman family as a full-fledged member.

Living the Dream

College in the U.S. was not possible for a variety of reasons, and Gideon returned to Israel to serve his mandatory military service. This allowed him time to prepare himself to pursue the dream of playing professional basketball in Israel. He had also developed an idea of starting a basketball sports academy that had formed during his days in Korea. The experiences of living in Kentucky with the Bantermans and working his way through the many disappointments of not playing regularly fueled his passion to make it in professional ball and give back to his community.

Gideon started university online and played university basketball while serving in the military, beginning his journey to the Israeli Basketball League. Shortly after being discharged from the military he was able to sign his first contract in Division 2. He became a veteran player in the Israeli league while simultaneously finishing his university degree in business.

Overlapping all of this was the development of a basketball sports training academy that had started as a part-time business and blossomed as Gideon's playing career wound down. And, the Bantermans continued to be a big part of his life. They called every three months and visited several times in both the U.S. and Israel. The circle was now complete as Gideon learned to pay it forward through his new business venture.

Three lessons of servant leadership have been part of the journey the Bantermans and Gideon have taken:

1. Gideon's story has been about building capacity in a person. Without the Bantermans' willingness to go beyond the bounds of their jobs to provide Gideon with an opportunity in the U.S., he would not have fulfilled his potential.
2. The Bantermans delighted in Gideon's successes, which has encouraged him to give more of himself to his work and community.
3. Ultimately, Gideon learned that he needed someone to believe in him for him to become a servant leader who would pour into others whom he served.

QUESTIONS FOR REFLECTION

- Have you ever taken mentees under your wing and guided them to reaching their full potential?
- What is an advantage to overcoming significant setbacks in fulfilling a goal or dream?
- Does your school have international students, and if so, how are they supported in their life goals?

FURTHER READING

Center for Teaching and Learning. (2019). *The Western guide to mentoring graduate students across cultures*. London, Ontario, Canada. http://www.uwo.ca/tsc/purpleguides.html

Slawinski, F. (2021). *The assessment of the Bain Inspirational Leadership Model in a Finnish media agency*. https://inside,arcad.fi/kultur-och-med

12

"Feed" Your People

Kelly Odell

The best test as a leader is: Do those served grow as persons; do they become healthier, wiser, freer, more autonomous, more likely themselves to become leaders?—Robert K. Greenleaf

Sao Feng lies on the deck, bloody, a long sharp shard of wood buried in his chest.

Elizabeth: Sao Feng?

Sao Feng: Here. Please. (removes the rope knot pendant he wears) The Captain's Knot. Take it. (she hesitates) So you'll be free! Take it! I must pass it on to the next Brethren Lord.

Elizabeth: Me?

Sao Feng: Go in my place to Shipwreck Cove.

(She takes the pendant. Tai Huang bursts through the door. Sounds of fighting follow him into the cabin—)

Tai Huang: Captain! The ship is taken! We cannot—(He pulls up short, takes in the scene. Sao Feng, mortally wounded, bleeding, whispers something low to Elizabeth, who listens intently.)

Sao Feng: Calypso . . . (he dies in Elizabeth's arms)

Tai Huang: What did he tell you?

Elizabeth: (holds up the pendant, now hanging around her neck) He made me Captain.

(Tai Huang turns angrily and returns to the deck.)

(Elizabeth steps onto the deck—littered with bodies, cannon smoke hanging in the air. Sails ripped to shreds. Moans from injured sailors. Huang follows behind her. The Flying Dutchman, with its contingent of encrusted crewmen, swarm onto the ship, rounding up terrified sailors. Two crewmen grab Elizabeth and Huang and put swords to their throats.)

Tai Huang: (to Elizabeth) You will never be my Captain!

(Commodore Norrington, strides forward, surveying the damage. He lifts his eyes—and sees Elizabeth. They embrace. Davy Jones steps past them, questions a lineup of sailors.)

Davy Jones: Who among you do you name as Captain?

Tai Huang: (points quickly at Elizabeth) Captain! Her!

(Other sailors quickly chime in, point. Norrington looks at Elizabeth, surprised.)

Norrington: Tow the ship. Take the sailors to the brig.

Davy Jones: You heard the Admiral!

Norrington: The Captain may have my quarters.

Elizabeth: No thank you, sir. I prefer to remain with my crew.

(She moves to follow her crew, being led away.)

Later that night—Flying Dutchman—Brig

(Elizabeth's eyes open at the sound of the jail door opening. Norrington is there.)

Norrington: Be quiet. This way. Hurry.

(Sao Feng's crew members look to Elizabeth. She nods, and they move past.)

—*Pirates of the Caribbean: At World's End*, screenplay by Ted Elliott & Terry Rossio, Green Revision (January 31, 2006)

It just so happened that just a couple of days before Marion watched this movie for the millionth time, she had read a section of Baruti K. Kafele's book, *The Principal 50*, where he discusses how to know if you are leading your team effectively. Two questions (among nine) he says we should ask ourselves are, "Will they [my team] go the extra mile for me? Will they sacrifice for me?" These scenes from *Pirates of the Caribbean: At World's End* jumped off the screen and smacked Marion in the face. Watch what happens when Elizabeth models how to get your team on your side.

Elizabeth was named as the crew's leader, but the crew was angry and would not follow her, even called her out as Captain hoping she would be killed by Davy Jones. But, when she was offered nice quarters during her captivity and refused in order to stay with her crew, their perspective of her changed. She showed them that she was one of them. Then, when it was time to escape they waited for her to lead them to safety. By the end of the movie she was standing on the rail of the ship, with crew from many different pirate ships, giving one of those monologues that pumps up the army and entices them to give their all in the battle they are about to fight. And every crew member on that ship followed her commands. This is servant leadership.

Marion never wanted to be a school leader. Let's back up, she never wanted to be a teacher, she never wanted to live in Kentucky, and she never wanted to be a principal. All of which she did or is doing now. But when the door opens and you feel yourself being pushed through it, you can dig your heels in all you want, but you are going through that door.

Marion went straight from the classroom, when the pandemic of 2020 hit, to the principal's role in a different district when the pandemic was in full swing. You can say it was a baptism by fire. But her main goal during that first year was to keep the teachers going and surviving—that was it. And she drew upon everything she had learned about being a servant leader and tried to put it into action. That first year was all about serving and encouraging.

Then her second year as a principal hit. Everyone was back in school full-time, and she had a team that only knew her as the one who sent heartfelt inspiring emails and threw as many sweet treats at them as she could. But it was time to start working on improving instruction. She laid out all the plans she had for them to implement, trained them on what she expected them to do, and made sure she walked through every classroom at least once every three to four weeks. She knew what she was doing and was ready to take charge and get things done. But no one could have anticipated what they faced.

The pandemic had much more of a social-emotional impact than was expected. Teachers were trying to meet Marion's expectations but were ministering to students that were depressed, detached from a structured system, and apathetic towards learning. The teachers themselves were going through their own post-traumatic stress that was inhibiting them from being able to give their best efforts in the classroom. And Marion was at a loss. She had not experienced this as a teacher. She could not connect with what they were going through. She tried to push them forward, but in the process, she was losing touch with reality and, in turn, losing relationships she had built with her team.

Marion was not who she wanted to be for her team and kept feeling the pull to get back to being the servant leader she was trained to be. She needed to step off the sled, where she was yelling, "Mush!" and grab a harness, attach herself to the gang line, and pull alongside everyone else. So, the next steps were to figure out how to do that.

As the teacher complaints about specific needs continued to grow, Marion's assistant principal (AP), instructional coach, and school counselor began to discuss with her how to address all the issues. To begin, they had two classes that were really struggling with behavior management. The AP and Marion took three days and spent entire blocks with the teachers in those different classes to help model some ways they could improve student behavior. They had multiple meetings where they encouraged and guided the teachers; and they made a plan that provided everyone with more confidence about the rest of the year.

But the inappropriate language and interactions amongst their hormonal preteens was becoming intolerable. The male AP worked with her and together they separated the boys and girls in that grade and had a heart-to-heart discussion about sexual harassment and inappropriate language and behaviors. The cafeteria monitors were ready to throw their hands up and let the students take control of the lunchroom. The AP and Marion dedicated themselves to lunchroom duty for an entire week to get everyone back on track and develop a monitoring system that worked effectively.

When it came to observations, they threw walkthrough forms out the window beginning in March and put on their cheerleading hats. They still visited each classroom every three to four weeks, leaving only encouraging notes with specific positive feedback to let the teachers know they saw the effort they were putting forth in the classroom.

But the *pièce de résistance* was bringing out the popcorn machine at a staff meeting. Suddenly, there were smiles and giggles, practical joking, and a sense of a weight being lifted off everyone's shoulders. Ding, ding, ding! Marion had not been feeding her people! That sounds ridiculous, but just taking the time to wheel a cart to everyone's door with a Little Debbie snack cake and a fun drink makes their day. She had not done that since early in the school year. You better believe she planned a snack cart or way to feed them every month for the rest of the year.

Little acts of kindness and getting down in the trenches with teachers is all it takes to let them see you care about them, instill their trust in you, and, before you know it, they will be fighting every battle with you.

QUESTIONS FOR REFLECTION

- How can you learn what your staff truly needs?
- What plan will you implement to meet those needs?
- Who are the people that can help you meet those needs?

FURTHER READING

Kafele, B. (2019). *The principal 50: Critical leadership qualities for school-wide excellence.* Association for School Curriculum and Development.

Kafele, B. (2020). *The assistant principal 50: Critical questions for meaningful leadership and professional growth.* ASIN: B088C1WBFM.

13

Changing the School's Positivity Image

William Sims

The best leaders are clear. They continually light the way, and in the process, let each person know that what they do makes a difference. —Robert K. Greenleaf

When Thomas was hired as the head principal of his large middle school after being the assistant principal the previous two years, he knew very well that he had an imposing task to undertake. The middle school, of which he now was the leader, ran the gamut of all types of students, from the impoverished to the upper middle class. The school's morale and image had taken some hits lately and improving faculty and staff morale was compounded by a need to bolster student morale and positivity as well. While Thomas knew the task in front of him was daunting, he was committed to improving not only the public image of his school, but the students' perceptions of the school and themselves, as well.

Thomas decided that he would need to attack morale and school-wide positivity issues from three different approaches. First, the teachers needed assurances that they not only mattered, but that they were already successful and vital to future student successes. Teacher achievements must be recognized and celebrated. Second, the students needed to be recognized and celebrated for all their efforts and achievements. Finally, and the most important aspect for establishing positivity and morale, the public must be made aware of the great successes that his middle school was having. In most cases, parents, and especially the public, in general, had very little idea of the many wonderful achievements going on at this school.

ADDRESSING FACULTY MORALE

To address the teacher morale issue, Thomas sent out surveys to the teachers, asking them what they needed to be successful. The questions asked were not relegated to tools and resources only, but more importantly he asked the questions related to the nontangible items that they needed to be successful teachers. Responses were gathered, organized, and prioritized. With a compilation of concrete and abstract needs and wants, Thomas began the school year with an unrelenting dedication to see that he would not only do everything within his administrative authority to give his teachers what they needed to be successful in the classrooms but to reach their professional goals as well.

After tallying and analyzing the results from his faculty, Thomas began the year fulfilling the requests of the teachers for resources needed. Being mindful of the school's budget, all the spending that he approved in the beginning of the year went toward resources that teachers felt they needed for a successful teaching year. Of course, not every request was granted, but the teachers genuinely appreciated all the efforts made by Thomas to obtain everything that he could for his teachers. Being persistent in his requests to his central office also netted additional resources that his school could not have purchased on its own budget alone.

Because Thomas had gone to every length possible to acquire what his teachers had requested, they responded very well, working diligently to utilize the resources and tools that he had secured for them. He made it a point to not stop there, but to check in regularly with each teacher to gauge the effectiveness of the programs, tools, and resources he had provided. He found that by doing these observations and leaving notes or sending short emails with simple messages such as, "You are doing a great job with this resource! You are awesome!" greatly improved teacher motivation and morale. The teachers knew that he was one with them, being a servant leader for them.

RECOGNITION OF STUDENTS

The second of the three issues that Thomas believed he must correct for his school was that of recognizing, awarding, and building the confidence of the students. He began with the goal of recognizing as many of the students in the school as possible, for all types of academic and character efforts. He instituted a "Positive Word of the Week," which he would announce and give the definition and examples of each day of the week. He would then ask each teacher to submit at least two students that embodied that word's spirit. On Fridays, he would read off the list of 20–30 students' names that had been submitted to recognize their positivity and influence in the school. All these students received a certificate of accomplishment.

After seeing how well the "Positive Word of the Week" program was progressing, Thomas realized another way to recognize even more students. All students in his school took a fall, winter, and spring progress monitoring assessment in math and reading. Thomas asked his teachers to submit names of students who not only performed at high academic levels on these assessments, but to also submit the names of several students in other categories that would realize effort and gains on the assessments. In this fashion, not only would students be recognized as being an "academic high-flyer," but every student who gave a genuine effort, despite their academic level, would be recognized as well.

This program of recognizing student achievement and effort became very successful, and created a positive, energetic culture among the students. However, Thomas knew he could do more to recognize and award every student. Adding to the positive word of the week and the three progress monitoring awards and recognition opportunities, Thomas asked his English language arts and math teachers to create categories for their computer-based enrichment classes that involved students working on their own levels in reading and math. With these categories generated by the teachers, even more students were being recognized during the morning announcements!

At this point, Tim, the school's guidance counselor, and Rich, the first assistant principal, approached Thomas and wanted to do even more to reward, recognize, and encourage students to do their best. Both Tim and Rich were involved in local businesses and groups that donated various items. Soon, both men were unloading truckloads of various new items to give to students who were being recognized for achievement and effort. Suddenly Thomas's school was giving out hats, T-shirts, sweatshirts, basketballs, soccer balls, and a multitude of items that middle school students were overjoyed to have.

INFORMING THE COMMUNITY

For his final aspect, and what he felt was the most vital, of the three-pronged approach to tackling the school's positivity and perception issue, Thomas wanted the parents, guardians, and the whole community to know about and join in the celebration of recognizing all the many wonderful experiences taking place in the school. Teachers were achieving greatness. Students were achieving greatness. The school's culture and climate were transforming in a much-needed direction. Now, the community needed to see and hear about what great things the faculty and students were producing in the school!

Thomas's school needed to get the positive information disseminated to the community, and the local paper was not the answer. In today's world of instantaneous information, there was a quicker and much better way, such as texting, social media, and a web link. Enlisting the aid of his second assistant principal Harrison, who was a former part-time reporter and photographer for the local newspaper, Thomas went to work to create a weekly newsletter that would be posted to the school web page, Facebook, Twitter, and most importantly, texted and emailed to every parent and guardian at his school.

The school newsletter, filled with applause, praise, and the celebration of positivity for the students and the school, was a success beyond Thomas's original expectations. The full-color newsletter resembled a regularly published online newspaper! It was a labor of love that Thomas found himself enjoying more and more during each week's publication, despite the enormous amount of extra time before and after school that he spent putting it together. While Thomas and Harrison had considerable hours compiled in each edition, a very minimal amount was required of the faculty, only the emailing of the recommended names for recognition and any pictures that they could share of their students.

Included in each newsletter with pictures and names were three students, one from each grade level, selected by the guidance office as "Students of the Week." Also, in each edition, four to five "Student Reps" from each of the nine school teams were pictured and named. In this way, every student in the school would be in at least one edition of the newsletter. Additionally, each grade-level team was featured on a rotating basis, enabling each team's teachers to submit pictures of their students in "academic action," as well as photographing students having a good time at school.

The newsletter also featured clubs, athletics, and other extracurricular activities in which the students participated. Photos and stories of the Art Club, Kindness Club, Board Games Club, Foreign Languages Club, and Cause for Paws were regulars in nearly every edition. Students that had achievements outside of school in non–school sponsored events were included with their stories, highlighting their successes in the county and state fairs, Boy Scouts, and Girl Scouts, to name a few. Other accomplishments, not officially associated with the school, were also regular items in the newsletter.

The regular sports section, led by Assistant Principal Harrison, would rival any newspaper coverage of Division I athletic programs. As the newsletter featured only one school, the sports section was a robust collection of photos of all the middle school student athletes in their games and competitions. Stories, photos, and features highlighted the positive efforts and work, while also calling attention to the positive way all the teams competed weekly.

The reception of the newsletter by the public was instantaneous and affirming. Regular comments on Facebook, Twitter, and emails regularly thanked the school for celebrating the students and bringing to the community all their wonderful accomplishments. With social media being a place where typically more negative comments usually overwhelm the positive regarding schools, the opposite effect was happening. People were now offering generous amounts of positive praise for the school!

As with most initiatives that are successful, Thomas had invested a considerable amount of time and effort into assuring that his faculty had the tangible and nontangible resources and mindset to be effective in their positions. A significant amount of extra time had to be put into creating the weekly newsletter, recognizing the students with a diverse mix of accolades. But the rewards of this effort were well-worth every minute. To be able to serve the school's faculty and students in this capacity was a joy to Thomas.

It should be noted that the servant leadership roles Counselor Tim and assistant principals, Rich and Harrison, added to the school dramatically increased the effectiveness of the three-point plan that Thomas envisioned. As Tim was very fond of saying, "Teamwork makes the dream work." Although a cliché, it proved to be a real component of Thomas's endeavor to serve the students and faculty of his school. Servant leadership often involves including a small group of like-minded professionals with the same goal of serving for student success and recognition.

The amount of time and effort that Thomas gave included many before and after school hours. The almost endless list of activities for a principal of a large school consume most of the time during the day, leaving only those hours when students and faculty are not in the building to complete the tasks needed to be successful in the three areas that Thomas assumed to better serve his school. While the newsletter was the one that demanded the most time and attention, the success that it provided his school proved to be worth all the extra time to improve the culture and climate for the students at his school.

QUESTIONS FOR REFLECTION

- Why is it important to involve the faculty in decisions that affect the school?
- What are some other ways in which student successes could be championed by a caring school administrator?
- Thomas's servant leadership example involves some other people from his administration team. Why is this important?

FURTHER READING

Burgess, S. & Houf, B. (2017). *Lead like a pirate: Make school amazing for your students and staff.* Dave Burgess Consulting, Inc.

Wiseman, L., Allen, L., & Foster, E. (2013). *The multiplier effect: Tapping the genius inside our schools.* Corwin.

14

Developing a Team

Myram Brady

The pessimist complains about the wind. The optimist expects it to change. The leader adjusts the sails. —John Maxwell

Megan was raised in her family to be strong and independent. She had strong leaders in her life that she admired—they led, and she followed. As she got older, she found herself being more of a team player than necessarily a leader. Whatever anyone needed, no matter how difficult it might be or how many other things were on her plate to which she committed, Megan just wanted to be able to help. To this day, there is that feeling in her that whatever she can do to be helpful, she should do it, no matter how exhausting it can become. Being a team player ultimately put her in the career of teaching, and she loved it and her students. There was a passion, and soon leadership took a hold of her life.

In a small K–8 school and the youngest educator on staff when she first started, Megan had incredible teachers all around her that were strong leaders. It was not long though, or so it seemed, that those teachers were ready to retire, and new teachers were stepping into their positions. Megan loved her school, and what they did, and how they did it. So when presented with a leadership role in the intermediate hallway, she jumped at it, even though she really did not understand the concept of servant leadership at that time.

Megan was doing what she had always observed modeled by her previous leaders, which was just being the leader and expecting everyone to follow that lead. What had worked had worked well, and she did not see the urgent need in allowing others to have a say and be creative to make a difference. At this point she was still at the place in her life where that was enough of a leadership role for her. She did not really look to go any further into deeper personal leadership development.

After several years, more turnover occurred, including a principal change. Two principals later, within just a couple of years, and Megan's school was starting to feel the hurt and lack of consistency in leadership. Some principals were coming in and either trying to change everything into the way they thought would work best or just focusing on what one or two thought would be good. At this point Megan realized that if she wanted the school to reach its full potential, she would need to push her comfort level and look into administration. She had always been one to say that you cannot complain if you do not contribute.

> *If you are not helping to make it right, then stop complaining about it being wrong.*—Unknown

It was when Megan started back in school for her administration courses that she was introduced to servant leadership. Throughout the process of reading and studying about this leadership "lifestyle," she realized that was what she wanted to do. It was different than the leadership style that she had experienced, and she could see that it could impact so many. As she read more and more stories and examples from the servant leadership literature, she became inspired and excited.

Megan began to realize that servant leadership is being a part of the process, not the head of the process. Within a short time, a position opened up at the high school for a Freshman Coordinator, and Megan decided that it was the right time and place to try something new.

> *Great leaders don't set out to be a leader . . . They set out to make a difference. It's never about the role, but always about the goal.*—Lisa Haisha

With some people, like Megan, when you move to a position of power, even those important things that you learned and admired can be easily forgotten or put aside for fear of making a mistake. After moving to the new position in November, many people approached her and wanted to give her advice on how she should do her job. She had done a lot of research on how to run a successful Freshman Academy, and although she welcomed their ideas, there was a small part of her that felt she was weak if she did not assert herself in the position. But she could not have been more wrong, and it did not take long for her to realize the impact.

As February approached and the grades were soon to be posted, Megan recognized that many of the freshmen were failing classes, and her nine teachers were very frustrated and overworked with trying to help the students.

She had continued with the weekly team meetings as her previous predecessor had done. She met and discussed common assessment data and student progress, leaving the meeting most of the time feeling defeated.

Megan was going into the classroom completing observations and offering suggestions, but that was the extent and she soon realized it was not cutting it. At this point in her short career as an administrator, she felt that she was accomplishing nothing in her job and neither her teachers nor her students were benefiting. When she had taught in the classroom, she had a relationship with her students and they worked hard for her, even those that struggled excelled in their own way. But that was elementary, and this was high school, and students are very different, or are they?

Megan was still being mentored as part of her administration certification, and it was during one of those meetings that she began to discuss how she felt in her position. Her mentor was very aware of the school Megan came from prior to the high school, and the culture she had experienced there as a highly skilled teacher. As they talked and she revealed how important relationships were to her, she was reminded of a book that she had read in one of her classes on servant leadership. She realized that what she was doing was not allowing anyone to be successful, and she was going to have to make some changes. But if she truly wanted to embrace this change, she could not complete it by herself. She was going to have to hear some hard truths from her teachers.

Everyone wins when a leader gets better.—Bill Hybels

As Megan looked for answers, she started turning to those that believed and lived by the principal of servant leadership. On her journey, she started researching through reading, watching TED Talks, and looking up successful leaders. She was still feeling a high level of defeat when she discovered Bill Hybels quote, "Everyone wins when a leader gets better." Her first step was to get better, but she still really was not sure how to accomplish it, because at this point not only did she have to get better, she had to get buy-in from her team.

Megan knew that building relationships between her teachers and students would show success, but being a math teacher, she realized that knowing the answer does not mean that you can solve the problem. If she wanted everyone to be successful, she was going to have to step away from everything she had known and seen as a leader and realize that asking for help and working with her teachers was not a sign of weakness or not knowing how to do her job.

People don't buy what you do; they buy why you do it. And what you do simply proves what you believe.—Simon Sinek

Megan started researching best practices when someone approached her with an idea. A neighboring county was working with their high school on building relationships through a grant and wondered if Megan would be interested in applying for the same grant. She spoke with a person from the company to learn more about the program. She felt this could help her find an answer, but there was a lot required of the program. She would be asking her teachers on top of their teaching, planning, and other duties to do this as well. The reality was that it was not just about Megan. She had to think about "we."

But Megan started to doubt her idea and basically just a lack of confidence, so she went to her husband to vent. She thought he would see her point of view and side with her. Well, guess what, he did not! His response was somewhere along the lines of, "So you thought this job would be easy and just fall into place for you?" He stated that Megan had to believe in herself and do what she felt was right.

Megan felt awful. Her husband had more confidence in her than she had in herself, and was not having confidence a prerequisite to doing her job?! She went back to the drawing board and found Simon Sinek. At that moment he said just what she needed to hear. Sinek stated, "People don't buy what you do; they buy why you do it. And what you do simply proves what you believe."

Megan realized that when she talked to her teachers and other administrators at her school, she did not need to approach the work as what needed to be done but why building relationships will make the difference.

> *Be credible-leading with the heart-consider the other person's situation: Encourage an environment to experiment—you can have many failures; Create an environment of psychological safety; Be a servant leader-listen, show compassion-ask for feedback.*—Adapted from Liz Theophille

To be a servant leader you have to be willing to manage psychological safety by taking risks and allowing those with whom you work to be able to give feedback to help you understand their point of view, which also allows them to feel their point of view is supported. Wow, that was hard to swallow! That meant that if Megan wanted to make a difference, she was going to have to be intentional and vulnerable.

So, Megan met with her teachers and explained that there was a problem with students' attendance, grades, and behavior to the point they were not being successful and would not by prepared to move on to their sophomore year, and more likely continue to struggle. Then she waited and listened to what her teachers thought. Slowly they started talking about individual students. A teacher would share what a student was experiencing, and another teacher would reply that they had no idea that was happening. What was supposed to be a 30-minute meeting after school turned into almost two hours, and Megan's team realized they did not really know their students and their needs. Until those were addressed, there would be little long-term academic success.

At the end of the meeting, Megan presented the program from the other school with which she had been impressed and asked the team to consider it. She explained the WHY of what she thought the team should do and not the WHAT. And, she listened to what her teachers said they needed most, which was more discipline support and more communication with students. For the first time since taking her new role, Megan felt that she and her team could make a difference and create relationships with their students. She felt different as a leader, and it felt good.

Megan's team made the decision to work together and receive training on the new program. They also decided to listen to each other, and as her teachers grew, Megan found new ways to support them. The one main point that Megan knew for sure from her years of being a teacher leader, and with this new adventure, was that she never asked anyone to do anything that she did not do herself. As a leader, her team needed to see that she was willing to roll up her sleeves and do the hard work too. So, she and her team trained together, and she rotated around to different rooms, helping with activities and working with both teachers and students. It was not easy, but the team was soon able to see the why and the answers themselves.

Student grades started going up. Students were answering more questions in class because they felt comfortable with the teachers and the other students with whom they worked. Attendance started getting better, and behavior started to decrease. Teachers had a little more prep work, but not as much stress with trying to play catch up with the students.

Megan had never been prouder of her teacher team. They took everything to the next level because they realized they were not doing it because Megan was making them. Together, they took ownership and were seeing progress. Together they were making a difference. Throughout the process Megan realized that being a leader could be scary, because to make a difference she had to try things that might fail. There were strategies she and her team tried that did fail, and they had to account for those, but they were in it together. Megan finally found her leadership fit.

Leadership is not wielding authority—it's empowering people.—
Becky Brodine

QUESTIONS FOR REFLECTION

- Initially, why was Megan struggling in her new role?
- What was here "aha" moment?
- What did she have to "give up" in order for her team to "grow up"?

FURTHER READING

Sinek, S. (2011). *Start with why: How great leaders inspire everyone to take action.* Portfolio Publishing.

Theophille, L. TED Talk (2020). How to lead from the heart. Chief Technology Transformation Office at Novartis. +Liz+Theophille&view=detail&mid=BAE9C873F0DC3680CFCABAE9C873F0DC3680CFCA&FORM=VIRE&safeSearch=strict&adlt=strict

15

When It Rains, It Pours

Laura Beth Hayes

Life has many ways of testing a person's will; either by having nothing happen at all or by having everything happen at once. —Paulo Coelho

We have all heard or used the expression, "When it rains it pours." Some days, especially in school administration, it should, perhaps, be revised to, "When it rains it is a monsoon." The calm, structured days always seem to be paralleled with days that are far more overwhelming and intense. It is in these times that we find ourselves faced with a crossroads. Servant leaders might panic and succumb to the pressure or dig deep for resiliency and strength.

One of the challenges of leadership is to balance authenticity and servant leadership. We must be able to be "real," yet also a beacon of peace and comfort when the world begins to crumble around the students and staff. This somewhat supernatural feat can only be developed and practiced in the face of adversity. Simply put, you must grab your best umbrella, stick on your rain boots, and trudge forth into the rain.

It all started when Mary woke up that morning. Her text messages were already stacking up, informing her of who was going to be absent due to COVID. The virus had really attacked her little school, impacting nearly a dozen employees, including the head principal. Over the last two weeks, nearly 20 staff members had been sick or were on quarantine due to family illnesses. Substitutes were scarce, and it was often a game of Tetris each morning to determine who could fit where for each hour of the day. Nearly 100 students were absent, and the stack of contact tracing paperwork was larger than ever. As she drove to school that morning, the clouded darkness cast an ominous shadow over the school—almost a foreshadowing of the day that loomed ahead.

Summoning her courage and positivity, Mary exited her car and walked into the building with a forced smile under her mask. As assistant principal, it was her duty to lead the school in her principal's absence. She had only been on the job for a few months and was still working to establish and build trust among the staff. "I can do this," she thought, as she crossed the threshold and prepared to be the rock that everyone expected.

As the morning unfolded, the usual hum of the school, buses, and car drop off line filled the hallways as students and staff entered a building that felt more like a war zone than a school. While other schools in the district were holding strong with their COVID numbers, this particular school had been hit extremely hard. Teachers felt overwhelmed in classrooms with so many students absent. Many teammates were throwing together plans for a colleague, and students were returning feeling anxious, tired, or lost from days spent at home.

Before the pledge was even recited, two more staff members tested positive, as well as two staff's children. Nearly fifteen other students were being "tested to stay" and the phone was ringing every few minutes with new cases and new quarantines. At one point, Mary packed up her essentials and camped out in the main office foyer, as the secretaries could not keep up with the incoming phone calls. Stacks of quarantine papers and charts for the many return-to-school scenarios littered the table where she sat—alongside hand sanitizer, caffeine, and an ink pen she nervously clicked.

The district called to offer help, but the thought of restructuring pawns throughout the chess board seemed more difficult than playing the daily game of using the servant-hearted staff already adjusting. Plus, now was not the time to wave the white flag. Mary knew that if she appeared weak, desperate for help, or ready to "give up," the ship would start to sink. Teachers were already drowning in their emotional exhaustion and the burden of pandemic teaching. They did not need this surge of the virus to be the catalyst that would destroy them.

"Thank goodness for masks," Mary thought as she walked the hallways gritting her teeth and hoping that her eyes did not give away the concern inside. What if more staff members tested positive as the day went on? How would the school function with nearly one-fourth of the student body at home?

Parents were increasingly frustrated with confusing quarantine protocols; the community cases were soaring; and the hope that the pandemic was coming to an end shattered as this new variant brought widespread destruction. Fears of incorrectly completing a contact tracing form or not adequately enforcing mitigation efforts filled Mary's mind. She worried about her own family and what would happen if she became ill as well. Every cough, every sniffle, every student she passed added to her concern. She had to keep her anxious thoughts in check and move forward.

As the morning passed, the gray skies only began to thicken—both physically and figuratively. Snow, which had been predicted for that evening, was beginning to move into the northern areas of the large county. Rumors were starting to slowly circulate that decisions were going to be made by the Central Office staff. Mary sat, briefly, and tried to remember any conversations about early release. They had not experienced one in a few years, and she certainly had never led that scenario. Texts were exploding from staff and the principal as emails dinged in a tauntingly obnoxious manner.

Parents called more than ever, inquiring about early release options and wanting the "inside scoop" that had not been shared publicly. Bus drivers were getting anxious and frustrated with no information. Other parents called with statements they had read on social media. The cafeteria staff needed to know how to proceed. Mary enlisted help in order to keep up with the digital information bombardment and develop a plan should an official statement be issued. Revised lunch schedules, revised specials schedules, and communication with families all had to be prepped and loaded . . . ready for release. Once the official statement was issued, the school was ready and unleashed the thrown-together plan.

Mary sipped her soft drink more than usual as she took a deep breath and stated to her office manager, "Okay . . . we've made it this far in the day. What else could go wrong now?" Somewhere in the Ten Commandments of school leadership is the statement, *"Never say what else could go wrong, because it will happen."*

In between the chorus of the phone ringing and the voices of frantic parents concerned about the light snow that must have had the appearance of a blizzard beyond the campus, the custodian raced in shouting that a water pipe had broken and was flooding the maintenance room. The only solution was to shut off the water main to the entire school. So now, school was dismissing early, yet there were 50 minutes of the day left, with no restrooms and no running water. Mary's concerns of COVID earlier in the day now seemed like a distant memory.

Precipitation was literally pouring outside and inside the building. Mary began to make calls to maintenance, circulated the building to be sure all staff received the memo about no water, and continued to reassure the staff that they would make it through the next hour. As the last bus pulled away, Mary realized she had never eaten lunch. She sat down and looked out the window as the snow continued to fall on the wintry barren land. She made an all-call informing staff that they should go home for the day in order to be safe and cautious.

Staff members bustled about to their cars, some looking a bit shell-shocked from the day's events, while others simply sat around—exhausted. As she warmed up her lunch, Mary penned an email to the staff thanking them for their flexibility, patience, and support throughout a quite abnormal day. COVID paperwork from the morning still loomed beside her salad, as well as a stack of Post-it notes that represented her scattered mind.

Mary became a bit emotional as she reflected on the day and the sheer exhaustion of trying to remain positive, in control, and strong. Her inexperience had contributed to the challenge, yet she did not let it cripple her rise to action. Although she did not always know what she should do next, she focused on one crisis at a time, centering first and foremost on the needs of the students. Mary acknowledged the staff's feelings and needs, and always offered a solution or a plan. She acted instead of reacting. She did not let the rainy events wash her away. Instead, she relied on her own toolbox, the strength of her people, and rallied a tired and worn-down staff together to do what they knew best—take care of children.

Sometimes leadership is all about the well-planned and strongly developed activities designed to strengthen culture and climate. Other times, like that day, it was all about Mary taking on the weight of the pouring rain and shielding the school with her umbrella. Servant leadership is sometimes a physical effort—cleaning up behind students at lunch, checking the building after a storm, or covering a class for a teacher who needs a break. Other times, servant leadership is more emotional-based and requires mental strength. Leaders, like Mary, have to flex their servant muscles, but also have to flex their servant strength.

For Mary, that day of "monsoon" problems was a transformational lesson, one that could never be taught in a college textbook or lecture. She learned that some problems can be tackled one at a time, and others are tackled in collective moments. That day presented challenges that may or not be replicated; there will always be issues and some will be even more difficult. She discovered that hope and encouragement can be found on even the most daunting of days. Later that evening, Mary received two texts from staff members:

- "You're a ROCKSTAR! Thank you for being so calm and handling things with common sense! I truly appreciate you!!!"
- "In case no one has told you lately, thank you for all you are doing! Thank you for stepping in and stepping up, for being positive, for bringing some creative new ideas, and for being a genuinely authentic person. We may forget to say thanks, but it doesn't go unnoticed. Hope this week is calmer for you!"

Shepherding a staff is not all that different from nurturing a classroom. Adults need to know you care and will invest in their best interest, and they are counting on you to be there when they need you. That day, despite her insecurities, nerves, fears, and chaos, Mary was simply there. So, the next inevitable time that someone on staff states, "When it rains it pours," there might be a small voice in the leader's head saying, "We've got this. It'll be ok. Open up the umbrella and walk out into the rain."

> *When it rains it pours. Maybe the great art of life is to convert tough times to great experiences: we can choose to hate the rain or dance in it.*—Jean Marques

QUESTIONS FOR REFLECTION

- Has your school ever been caught in a situation where the "perfect storm" hit, without warning?
- Is your staff well trained in handling a crisis situation when the lead principal is out of the building?
- Why is it important to follow the chain of command when there are multiple complex issues happening all at once?

FURTHER READING

Bridwell-Mitchell, E.N. & Lant, T. (2013). *Be Careful What You Wish For: The Effects of Issue Interpretation on Social Choices in Professional Networks.* https://doi.org/10.1287/orsc.2013.0840

Snyder, K., & Giella, M. (2013). *Developing principals' problem-solving capacities.* Association Supervision of Curriculum and Development.

16

30 Minutes

Michael W. Kessinger

On an important decision one rarely has 100% of the information needed for a good decision no matter how much one spends or how long one waits. And, if one waits too long, he has a different problem and has to start all over. This is the terrible dilemma of the hesitant decision maker.—
Robert K. Greenleaf

It was the start of the new school year and Rick was looking forward to another new beginning. The previous year he was moved from the classroom and assumed the duties of assistant principal (AP). It was an interesting move, as the previous assistant unexpectedly resigned his position and took a principal's job in another state. Being one of two individuals certified for the position, the Superintendent moved both into what was a single administrative role. Part of Rick's negotiation was he was able to remain the teacher of the single AP Computer Science class. He loved teaching, but the challenge of the administrative position was also something he felt he was prepared to face.

TENNIS COACH

Not only was Rick teaching one class and being one of the two assistant principals, he was also the tennis coach. When he started the team a few years earlier, he was faced with an additional challenge. Since tennis was not a revenue generating sport, there needed to be a watch on the amount of money spent by the team. One big expense was travel. So, another task Rick had to assume was driving the bus to the out-of-town tennis matches. Assuming that duty was a no-brainer as it would eliminate having to wait for a regular bus driver to get back to the high school after the regular run. Rick could load the team and leave right away. This would also get the team back home earlier in the night.

Playing tennis was something Rick had enjoyed in his college years. Participating on the community college team with his doubles partner, Gary, was a special part of his higher education experience. So, coaching the high school team allowed Rick to continue to hit the ball along with the opportunity to teach others the game of tennis. It was great going to the matches and encouraging his players to not only learn the game, but also to do their best. And, the conversations after the match, while getting something to eat, were rewarding to Rick. But he also learned a lot about his players, where they came from, their home life, their aspirations, and their struggles.

After one match, as the team arrived at a fast food restaurant to get something to eat, one player, Scott, said he was going to just stay on the bus and rest. Scott was a good player and really had a tough match that evening, so it was understandable he was tired. Another player approached Rick.

"You know why Scott doesn't want to come in here, don't you?" asked Stephanie. "He doesn't have any money." The kid's homelife was a struggle. Living with only his mom and three brothers, Scott did not always have the money to buy dinner. Rick went back out to the bus and carefully confronted his young player.

"Scott, you really need to get something to eat. It will help you gain your strength back. You had a good match, but you need to eat something."

"Coach, I'm just not in the mood to eat right now. I'll get something when I get home."

"Come on Scott. Come on in. I know why you don't want to eat. Here's $5. Get yourself something—now!"

"Coach, I can't take your money. I can't pay you back."

"Who said this was a loan Scott? Come on. Let's go in. I'm hungry too and I'm not going to eat if you do not. And who said anything about paying me back? Don't you know—teachers are rich!"

Getting off the bus and walking to McDonald's, Scott said, "Coach, thanks. You're the best."

"No Scott, you are the best. Now shut up and let's eat."

Rick always had some extra money just in case one of his players did not have the cash to eat. It was important to be a good coach but also to take care of his players' needs. The challenges of many of the students were things Rick had also experienced as a youth. It was his desire to help students as their needs required.

BUS DRIVER

About two months into the school year, Rick received a phone call telling him to come to the central office (this was before email, so a phone call was the only way to get messages to employees, parents, and district stakeholders). Arriving at the office, Rick was directed to the transportation director.

"Seems we have a problem. I'm needing a bus driver to take the Meathouse run. The driver quit because he got a job in the coal mines. Who can blame him? He'll be making a lot more doing that than $50 a day driving the bus. You interested Rick in taking this run over? You live right near there. Imagine how much you'll save on gas. You will be driving the bus to school and back home. What do you say? Fifty dollars a day is a lot of money and you're a young guy. You'll take it, right?"

The argument was persuasive, and the money would be helpful, Rick thought. "Sure, when do I start?"

"Tomorrow morning. You can get the bus at the elementary school. The keys will be in it."

After getting more of the details regarding the run, starting time, the route, and other particulars, Rick was now not only the assistant principal, and tennis coach, he was a bus driver. "Wonder how many more things I'll be doing here," he thought.

The Meathouse route was an interesting run. Rick learned that it would take around 45 minutes from the head of Meathouse to the elementary school, then another 15 to 20 minutes from the elementary to the high school. When asked about what time he would need to leave the house, the transportation director said, "Around 5:45 a.m. It will take you about 25 minutes to get to the first pickup spot, then around 45 minutes to get to the elementary school. You'll wait for the other buses and then take the older students to the high school. After that, you're done. Short and sweet."

Rick started to think about all of this. Start picking up at 6:10 a.m.; 45 minutes to get to the school—that's 6:55 a.m.; Wait for the other buses to arrive at the elementary; Transfer high school students to my bus and get them to the high school by 7:45 a.m. so they can eat breakfast. Sounds doable.

The first morning Rick did as he planned. He left his trailer at 5:45 a.m. and was sitting at the first house at 6:05 a.m. Slowly the three students came out of the house and got on the bus. All three sat in the first seat. Rick turned and said, "Good morning." He noticed immediately one of the kids was already fast asleep.

The route was a simple one, all on Meathouse Road. Luckily there were no coal trucks running so the narrow spots in the road were not an issue. Picking up students was easy. As they stepped onto the bus, Rick spoke to each group, saying, "Good morning." But one of the things Rick noticed was the bus was quiet. Very little talking was going on. Looking through the rear mirror, he could see the high school kids in the middle to back rows quietly talking to each other. But the little ones sitting in the front seats were not viewable from the mirror.

Once Rick arrived at the elementary school, he turned around. And to his surprise, the first few rows had children leaning on each other, sleeping. The older kids were quietly waking up the younger ones, helping them to get off the bus. It was 7:00 a.m. Rick thought, "This is crazy!" Stopping a high schooler, Rick asked, "Is it always like this?"

"Yeah, it's really early for some of these kids. Really hard."

Once unloaded, Rick saw that a few older students were still on the bus. "How long do we wait on the other buses?" Rick asked.

"They get here about 7:25 a.m., and then we leave for the high school."

Rick thought, "I'm waiting for 25 minutes? I'm going to fix this."

The next morning the same thing happened. Rick started picking up at 6:05 a.m., got to the elementary around 7:00 a.m., waited for the other buses, and then arrived at the high school at 7:45 a.m.

On the third day, a change was in the works. A note was given to each child as they got on the bus. "Make sure your mom gets this note. I will be picking you up 30 minutes later. Remember 30 minutes later. Don't forget—30 minutes later." Rick made the same announcement at each stop. "Tomorrow—I'll get here 30 minutes later."

Finally, at the elementary school, Rick stood up before anyone could get off the bus. "Tomorrow I will pick you up 30 minutes later. Stay in bed and sleep 30 minutes longer. Make sure your parents get the note I've given you. Remember, 30 minutes later."

The same announcement was repeated over and over on the afternoon run. Getting these students on the bus before it was necessary was just crazy, and there was no reason for them to have been getting up so early to catch a bus so it could arrive at the elementary school early.

On the fourth day, Rick arrived at the first stop at 6:35 a.m. He thought, "Good, I'm 30 minutes late." The first group of children came out of their house, but this time their mom came with them. As the kids got on the bus, the mom spoke, "Thank you. You don't know how happy my kids were that they got a little more time to sleep this morning."

The rest of the run went smoothly, and everyone made it to the bus at the new time. No child was left behind because of the change.

Arriving at the elementary school was also interesting. Before, Rick would see seats and rows of children sleeping. This morning the bus was full of kids chatting to each other. When he turned around, no one was sleeping—they were awake and talking. And the wait for the other buses was very short, no 30-minute wait for the buses to arrive to transfer high school students.

BUS IN THE DITCH

Returning kids home in the evening was always a nice time to listen to the day's activities. But it was also enjoyable to drop off the last three at their house so Rick could get back to his home. One time in his rush, he backed the bus a little bit too far and got it stuck in a ditch. "Oh gosh!" he yelled to himself.

Getting out, Rick walked to the first house—the Fletcher home. The youngest child, Sally, opened the door. "Mom, it's Mr. G, the bus driver." Rick's last name was not a common name for eastern Kentucky, so almost everyone just called him Mr. G.

"Can I help you Mr. G.?"

"Yes, it seems that I'm stuck in the ditch. Can I use your phone to call the bus garage?"

"We don't have a phone, but my husband can pull you out. But first, come in and have dinner with us."

"Thank you, but I can't do that. I appreciate the offer." It was not that Rick did not want to eat, because the meal smelled so good. He just did not want to take any food from this family.

"I insist. Come on in." At that moment, little Sally grabbed Rick's hand and said, "Come on Mr. G, eat with us."

The innocent pressure from Sally was enough for Rick to agree to come in. Sitting around the table, Sally right next to Rick, the mom said, "I hope you like soup beans. And we have peach cobbler for dessert."

"That sounds great."

During the meal, Mr. Fletcher was told of the situation with the bus, and he told Rick after they ate, he would get the bus out of the ditch.

The dinner was great and the peach cobbler was one of the best Rick had ever eaten. Sally talked non-stop the whole time. Rick did not know she could talk so much, as she was very quiet on the bus trip each day. The conversation was great, and Rick really enjoyed the country meal and hospitality.

Leaving to go to the bus, Mrs. Fletcher handed Rick a bag. "Here's a little something to take with you." Peeking in the bag, there was a Mason jar of soup beans and a Cool Whip container. "There's peach cobbler in the Cool Whip bowl. I saw how you really woofed that down. You must really like cobbler."

"Thank you so much. I'm going to really enjoy this. Thank you."

"No, thank you Mr. G for what you did. That extra 30 minutes really helps our kids. It was such a chore to get them going so early in the morning. Thank YOU!"

SEVEN YEARS LATER

It was the start of another new school year. Rick was standing at the door greeting students as they entered the building. It was always a time of seeing old students and then meeting the new ones. One girl came straight to Rick.

"Do you remember me?" she asked.

Rick quickly tried to recall if this was a returning student or a new one. "No, I'm sorry. I don't remember."

"I'm Sally Fletcher! You were my bus driver on Meathouse. You remember now?"

"Sally, it's been so long. After they hired the new driver for Meathouse, I just never went up there again. How are you doing?"

"I'm great. I'm in high school now and, well, it's high school. I'm going to tell mom that I saw you. Hey, do you remember the '30 minutes'? You said that a lot that one day."

Rick smiled. It had been a while, but that bus run was something that had to be fixed. "Yes, I remember that. I'm surprised that you do."

"Oh, I'll never forget. You have a great day Mr. G."

"Thank you Sally. You too."

Two weeks later, Rick was sitting in his office right before school started. There was a knock on his door. "Sally. Good morning. You need something?"

"Mr. G. My mom says 'Hi' and said to give this to you."

Handing Rick a bag, Sally turned and walked off saying, "Have a good day Mr. G."

Rick wondered and slowly opened the bag. Inside was a Mason jar and a Cool Whip container. He thought, "Oh no! It can't be." But it was—dinner.

QUESTIONS FOR REFLECTION

- What do we do to help meet the needs of others when they do not make it known what their needs are?
- What have you done that has made an impact in someone's life that you did not realize until years later?
- Who have you served in your career that you remember after years have passed?

FURTHER READING

Meador, D. (2019). *Role of principal in schools.* https://www.thoughtco.com/role-of-principal-in-schools-3194583#:~:text=1%20Student%20Discipline%20Chief.%20A%20large%20part%20of,Public%20Relations%20Point%20Person.%20...%207%20Delegater.%20

Parker, W. (2016). The 8 hats of a school leader: Principal matters. https://williamdparker.com/2016/06/14/mpm-026

17

What Servant Leadership Is and Is Not

Franklin Thomas

True understanding of a concept requires a consideration of what that concept is not.—Franklin Thomas

James was a director of student services for a small school district. It was about 4:00 p.m., with the end of the workday less than 30 minutes away as he sat in his office preparing to process three applications for the district's homebound program. This program was for students with short- or long-term physical or mental illness that prevented them from attending school in person. The program provided a teacher to visit the students' homes at least two times weekly to drop off work, provide instruction, and pick up work.

James had to ensure that the applications were complete and met the letter of the state law. He then had to notify several individuals about the applications and update the students' records. His plan was to begin this work and complete it the next day. But his work was interrupted when Robert, the school superintendent, entered.

Unfortunately, this visit was not social or about a routine work matter. The homebound applications were on Robert's mind too. He walked over to James's desk and soon saw his objective. He picked up the homebound applications, looked through them, placed one on top of the stack, and returned them back to James's desk. Robert then pointed to the application on top and said, "Expedite this one." Initially puzzled, James looked at the name on the application. The name was "Christopher," and then Robert's actions immediately became very clear. A few weeks prior, Christopher's father had been elected to the school district's board of education. After a brief pause, James replied, "I'll expedite all of them." After another brief pause, sufficiently satisfied, Robert smiled and walked out.

James's approach to which homebound application would be processed first and which student might begin receiving services first was based upon one thing—student need. This really *was not* about servant leadership, but rather just a logical approach. Robert's approach to which homebound applications would be processed first and which student might begin receiving services first was based upon one thing—his own needs and desires. This really *was* about servant leadership, the antithesis of servant leadership. At some point, a casual conversation between Robert and Christopher's father likely took a turn as follows: "Is everything going well with Christopher's homebound services? I made sure that the services started as quickly as possible."

The short pause before James's response to the superintendent was home to lots of quick thoughts . . . "I can't say 'no,' that's insubordination. I can't say 'okay,' because that hurts the kid who really needs to receive the services first."

"I'll expedite all of them" was not exactly what the superintendent wanted to hear, as evidenced by his pause, but it obeyed the directive and it ensured that services were not delayed for the neediest kid. James wrapped up a few tasks, locked his office door, signed out, and made the 10-minute drive home. All the time he was dismayed by those three words, "Expedite this one."

As quickly as his response to the superintendent came to mind, James's plan for the evening was formulated. He would eat supper, rest a bit, and then return to work and stay as long as it took to complete the processing of all of the applications. This would obey the directive from his superior and ensure that the neediest kids received services as quickly as possible.

In this brief account, James is a servant leader in that he placed the needs of the students above his need to more definitively comply with the directive of his superior. He placed the needs of the students above his need to have a relaxing evening at home. Robert was not the servant leader as he placed his need to score a point with the new board member above the needs of his most vulnerable students. To make matters worse for Robert, among the hundreds of thousands of words that he has spoken to James, the three words that he uttered that day did irrevocable harm to James's opinion of him as a leader. On this particular day, Robert took the wrong path to greatness. A leader's greatness is built upon the practice of serving other people (Spears, 2004).

James demonstrated a bit of servant leadership by giving up his relaxing evening at home to obey his superior while ensuring that appropriate services were not delayed to any student. This was admirable but just a drop in the bucket to James. He was no stranger to putting in lots of extra time on the job. This was the case for his current job, but much more so with his previous positions as a school assistant and later head principal.

As a school administrator, James was never late to work and liked to say that the principal should be the person to brew the first pot of coffee in the teachers' lounge. One of his first tasks was to raise the American flag in front of the school just after daybreak. No matter how busy the morning, he always made time to get on the school intercom to make announcements, offer a few words of wisdom, and introduce a student volunteer to lead the recitation of the pledge to the flag. His mornings were filled with paperwork, meetings, email, and telephone calls. No matter how heavy that load, he always found time to practice "managing by walking around." Lunchtime always found James standing in line with the students to eat in the school cafeteria. Afternoons were much like the busy mornings.

At the end of the school day, James was back on the school intercom with announcements. He ensured all students were on their school buses and signaled the buses to leave. He made sure that the students being picked up by their parents made it safely to their pickup point. His dismissal routine was completed with a quick walk of the building to be sure that all students had exited. Faculty could leave for the day 30 minutes after the students departed. James's faculty was very dedicated, but most were headed home around 4:00 p.m.

James, on the other hand, would visit a local restaurant for supper and then return to work for several more hours. His day ended with a walk of his school, inside and out, to be sure that everything was ready for the next day. He would then announce on the intercom, "If anyone is left in the building, call the office. The alarm will be set shortly." Very seldom did anyone respond. He turned out the lights, set the alarm, locked the doors, and drove 45 minutes to his home.

On many evenings there were events such as basketball games. The responsibility for supervising these events was split between James and his assistant. However, since James was usually already working late, he would often send his assistant home and take care of the duty himself. Those days wrapped up about 10:00 p.m. as James dropped off the admission gate money from the game at a local bank's night deposit. James's school had numerous sports teams and, while he could not attend all events, he did try to attend as many as possible. Sometimes, this even included away games.

James had a special interest in making his school building as comfortable and as inviting as possible. As he made his nightly rounds inside and outside the building, he could be seen picking up trash or fixing small maintenance issues. He had a drawer in his office containing tools, paint, cleaners, and other materials for quick maintenance projects. A water spot on the ceiling tiles or a little graffiti on the walls would not last until the next day on James's watch. Sometimes when the custodians got behind in the yard work, he would bring a weed trimmer and a change of clothes to school and help them catch up. He had a special desire to make the teachers' lounge a place where hard working staff could really relax for a few minutes. Out of his own pocket, he even purchased a massage chair for the lounge.

The end of a school year was a particularly busy time for James, but summer was near. Although he was contracted to work most of the summer, at least the first month or so was a bit slower paced. However, the last few weeks of summer were often the most time consuming as he saw to many details to ensure a smooth start to the new school year. This time of year would often see James working weekends. One July he worked 19 calendar days straight. He was actually contracted to work 240 days. His district operated on an honor system instead of having a method to verify that administrators worked all their contract days. While sitting in a meeting of other administrators from his district James once quipped, "Don't tell anyone at the district office, but last year I only worked 243 of my 240 contracted days."

This sounds like the story of someone who is a great servant leader. However, at some point that is a bit hard to pinpoint, as James began displaying something that servant leadership is not. He detested being away from his school. He would avoid attending trainings and other meetings whenever possible which stymied his professional growth. Even when he felt terrible, he essentially never took a sick day. One afternoon, James felt very feverish and had himself checked out by his school nurse. She said that his fever was the highest that she had ever measured in an adult and demanded that he go home. He refused because of an important meeting that he was chairing after school. When the nurse threatened to call James's wife, he left for home. He was a servant leader, but he was not stupid.

James's time spent at work obviously took away greatly from time spent with his wife and kids. Although his wife was supportive of his leadership style, his teachers jokingly referred to her as the "principal's widow" because she seldom saw her husband. James took little time for hobbies and continued to tend to school matters by phone while on his family's summer vacation. During the winter when the days were short, he would leave home before sunrise and return after dark. At one point he realized that he would go five days without seeing his home in the daylight. Of course, all that has been described had negative impacts on James's health. He is a great example of what servant leadership is and is not. It is not intended to be destructive to the leader. The trick may be in determining when the scales tip.

QUESTIONS FOR REFLECTION

- If, in a moment of weakness, you did something self-serving and detrimental to others, how would you feel the next day?

- How will you react to others who engage in actions that are the converse of servant leadership?
- Do you know someone who is a servant leader to the point that it may be destructive to them? What is your evidence? Is that person you?

FURTHER READING

Doshi, P. (2020). The power of shared decision-making through servant-leadership. https://www.scrum.org/resources/blog

Spears, L. (2004). *Practicing servant leadership*. Wiley Publishing.

Zhong, L., Qian, Z., & Wang, D. (2020). How does the servant supervisor influence the employability of postgraduates? Exploring the mechanisms of self-efficacy and academic engagement. *Front. Bus. Res. China* 14 (11). https://doi.org/10.1186/s11782-020-00079-1

18

Service

The Secret Ingredient to Successful Leadership

Carrie Ballinger

> *Rockcastle County Schools exist to educate, feed, and support our students.* —Carrie Ballinger

On Friday evening when the last family who had sought refuge at the Rockcastle County Warming Center was loaded into the Mount Vernon Fire Department truck to be returned to their home, tears of gratitude and thankfulness were shed. The devastating ice storm brought more to Rockcastle County than tragedy and distress. It brought an opportunity to serve and to demonstrate love, care, and compassion to a community in need.

When the harsh winter weather attacked the state of Kentucky, Rockcastle County was in the eye of the ice storm—receiving over an inch of ice, shutting down travel across the county, and knocking out power to over 75 percent of the county's homes and businesses. The temperatures dropped to below zero, and weather conditions were brutal. This scenario quickly turned into an emergency situation in which families were stranded without electricity, without an alternative heat source, and with no way to feed themselves or their families.

Many areas of the county were also without water, further compounding the distress that the community was experiencing. As the storm continued to pound the community, the distress worsened, and a state of emergency was declared for Rockcastle County. It truly was a state of emergency for many students and families of the school district.

Knowing the servant leaders that made up the Rockcastle County School team, "Absolutely!" was the answer given by Superintendent Carson when receiving a phone call from the Rockcastle County Judge Executive, informing her that a state of emergency had been declared. Rockcastle County Schools was asked to partner with the county and with the Rockcastle County Emergency Operation Center to open a Warming Center at Rockcastle County Middle School.

With a team that believed and lived the motto, "Rockcastle County Schools exist to educate, feed, and support our students," the decision to serve the school community and the community as a whole during their time of need was easy. The Rockcastle County School team sprang into action, and within an hour, the doors to the Rockcastle County Warming Center were opened.

A servant leader is called to love and to be of service to others, not only when times are easy, but also when times are tough. Being a servant first and a leader second defines servant leadership. Service, and specifically servant leadership, requires leaders to place others before themselves and lead by example, choosing to give rather than receive. Servant leaders focus on the well-being of the communities in which they live and serve. This is exactly what took place over the span of one week in a small rural community in Southeastern Kentucky, a focus on the well-being of a community in dire need of assistance.

As a group text went out to the district administrative team explaining the situation and seeking assistance, there was no surprise in the responses that were received.

"I'll meet you at the middle school in 30 mins."

"We just got a shipment of food two days ago, and there is extra water in the kitchen."

"I will get the parking lot cleared."

"If I get there before you, I will start setting up the cots."

"People will be cold. Do we have enough blankets?"

"I still have electricity. I will start fixing chili. People will be hungry."

"There is extra salt at the bus garage. I will get that for the sidewalks."

"The tarp is hard to get down on the gym floor. I will be right there to help get that down and set up the cots."

Every response that was received was a commitment to assist, serve, love, care, and put others before themselves. Knowing that these very people were without electricity in their own homes made the commitment to service even more remarkable. In a short span of time, these leaders along with the Rockcastle County Judge Executive and the Emergency Operations team had over 50 cots set up in the gym and were ready to receive friends and neighbors.

"Breaking News: The Rockcastle County Judge Executive and Rockcastle County Schools are opening a warming center at Rockcastle County Middle School for those without electricity. Food, water, showers, and transportation are available." As this emergency message was shared on the local radio station, across social media platforms, and on the Rockcastle County Schools website, families began pouring into the school.

As families began arriving at the school, it was a scene very similar to what would be imagined during war times. People were wearing layer upon layer of clothes, carrying small bags of their personal belongings, and were somewhat despondent. They were scared, cold, uncertain, and many were simply in shock. But they were warmly welcomed at the door, reassured, and helped to the gym by members of the school team. Once in the gym, each person was assigned a cot and given a warm blanket, a bottle of water, and a bag of snacks. Some people wanted to share their story, and the team listened. Some people wanted to be alone, and the team respected their wishes. Others slept, others needed medical attention, and others simply cried.

Part of being a servant leader is having the capacity to put other people, whether students, employees, parents, or community members, at the very top and putting oneself at the bottom. Leading with a service mindset, servant leadership requires uplifting and empowering others, showing humility rather than displaying harsh authority. A servant leader strives to develop trusting relationships with stakeholders, and the basis of these relationships is built upon stewardship. Stewardship is leading by example, modeling the culture the servant leader envisions. The phrase, "Never expect someone to do something you are not willing to do yourself," encapsulates the culture of an organization fueled by servant leadership.

In the midst of a fierce, winter storm, the servant leaders of the Rockcastle County school team suddenly found themselves serving as counselors, arranging emergency transportation, providing medical care, contacting health care providers, finding long-range housing for the homeless, coordinating services with first responders, planning and serving meals, sharing a listening ear, and making new friends. A small team willing to serve their community with love and compassion quickly turned a sterile warming center in a school gym into a home away from home for a community in need.

The power of love, compassion, and caring was a beautiful sight. After the people in the shelter began to warm, had a good night's sleep, ate several hot meals, and took a hot shower, a change began to occur. Those same people who had arrived at the shelter scared and despondent slowly began to smile again. They began to talk, socialize, share, make friends, and heal. They began to assist each other, care for one another, and treat the Rockcastle County Middle School like their home. In just a few short days, total strangers became dear friends, and a local disaster became an avenue for outreach and compassion.

Volunteers throughout the Rockcastle County community poured their hearts into service and showed great love to strangers who quickly became family. The entire community rallied behind feeding and ensuring the safety of their friends and neighbors in need. That week there were thirty-seven people served with love at the warming center. That week a renewed faith in humanity occurred. That week strangers became family, and servant leadership was modeled, and humility was on display.

On the third night of the warming center being open, an older gentleman was restless and pacing through the cafeteria during the midnight hour. When a member of the school team asked him to sit down to talk over a cup of coffee, the conversation quickly went to why.

"Why are you treating us all so kindly? Why are you leaving your own families to serve us? Why do you care? Why do you wait on us, making certain we are warm and well fed?"

During the conversation the man shared that he had never experienced this type of love before and that he was hesitant to go back to his home alone. He had witnessed a different way of life than he had ever experienced, and he wanted more. He referred to the school volunteers as angels and the warming center as Heaven. This is the epitome of servant leadership—putting the needs of others before yourself in a caring and compassionate fashion.

As the week progressed, it was heartwarming to see the distress and desperation in the eyes of the men and women staying at the warming center be washed away only to be replaced by a look of rest and calm. A peace flooded the entire center, and at that point, the school team knew we had successfully served our community. As homes across the county slowly began to have their electricity restored, our new friends began to leave the center to return to their lives. As families exited the school, tears flowed, and goodbyes were shared. It was a bittersweet week where total strangers and servants were brought together through tragedy—all returning to their separate lives abundantly blessed.

QUESTIONS FOR REFLECTION

- What traits, behaviors, and leadership qualities did this school team exhibit during the warming center event that would lead to enriching the culture of servant leadership within the organization?
- How do you think the servant leadership qualities displayed during this event shaped the community's view of the school district?

- How could the servant leadership qualities displayed during this event be transferred to the everyday operations of a school system?

FURTHER READING

Lynch, M. (2019). How servant leadership can transform your school district from the inside out. *The Edadvocate Newsletter.* https://www.theedadvocate.org

Stewart, J.G. (2017). The importance of servant leadership in schools. *International Journal of Business Management and Commerce*, 2(5).

19

The Milkman

Ann Burns

Children learn more from what you are than what you teach.—
W.E.B. Du Bois

Mr. Brown had been a part of the community for many years. He had joined the district from the local university during his student teaching semester and decided to build his career in this small, rural community. He and his wife had been hired as teachers and raised their family here. When he secured the opportunity to lead one of the elementary schools in the district, he jumped into the job with all the enthusiasm and confidence a young principal could have. His excitement for learning and students could not be contained and he and his school quickly outperformed many of the schools led by veteran principals in the district in student achievement. The other principals tried to learn his secret for developing teachers and students. But the secret was in plain view, his service to the profession and the people.

As the district assessment coordinator, Dr. Fireman, was working with all the building principals equally close, it was obvious that there was certainly something special in the way Mr. Brown interacted with his students and teachers. Arriving early to his school one morning, she watched as he assisted each bus with unloading and greeted each student by name. She could not resist asking, "How on earth do you remember 500 students' names?"

Mr. Brown responded, "Some days are easier than others," adding a quick laugh as he continued to assist a steady stream of five-and six-year olds off the bus.

Dr. Fireman thought quietly, "The students all seem so happy and ready for learning. What am I missing?"

Mr. Brown finished his bus duty, and the two administrators continued talking as they walked into the school building to talk about upcoming mandated testing. After reviewing the schedule, updating the testing rosters, securing the testing materials, and discussing any questions that needed to be reviewed, Mr. Brown looked down at his watch and gasped, "I need to be in the lunchroom—it is milk time."

Curiously, Dr. Firemen replied, "What is that?"

Pushing his chair away from his desk, Mr. Brown invited her to come join him. "You are in for a treat!" He quickly proceeded down the hallway.

The two entered the lunchroom, where a line of hungry students were beginning to form at the front of the serving station. Mr. Brown stood at the end of the line where students picked up their milk to go with their daily meal. As the line wound toward the two adults, you could hear the students' excitement as they exchanged informal conversations with the building principal. Dr. Firemen stood and watched the principal as he interacted with students while they moved through the lunch line and out to the cafeteria for their meal.

"How is your new baby sister, Eli?" Mr. Brown inquired as he sat a milk carton on Eli's tray. "Has your Mama gone back to work yet?"

"She cries a lot, Mr. Brown, but we are learning to adapt to it," Eli replied.

"It will get better, and she will settle in," Mr. Brown assured him.

"Did you get your homework finished for Mrs. Reynolds?" he asked the next student as he placed his milk carton on the tray.

The young man nodded his head and Mr. Brown commented, "That is a great job!" A huge grin spread across the young student's face as he exited the lunch line.

For the next hour, the administrators continued to place milk on each student's lunch tray and banter back and forth about random topics, all the while interacting with the cafeteria team and classroom teachers as they filtered through for lunch.

Dr. Firemen asked Mr. Brown, "How often do you assist with lunch service?"

Mr. Brown replied, "Every day I am in the building. It is crucial for me to check on my babies. It is important to me that the students, faculty, and staff know that I care about them personally—not for who they are, or what services they provide the school, but individually, as people. The best way to show that is to interact with as many students, teachers, parents, and staff as I can daily. The lunch line offers me a captured audience to check in on all my students. I try to engage with them every day. Passing out milk seems small, but to me, it is how I check in with families, both grown and young ones."

The young principal continued to interact with students as they came to the end of the lunch line and received their milk. "There are parts of the job that are not rewarding but passing out milk at lunch is one of the most rewarding things I do," he continued with a smile. Dr. Firemen made a mental note that the students were smiling, too.

As the day continued, Dr. Firemen visited other schools to discuss the upcoming mandated assessments, but failed to witness the personal interaction with students, faculty, staff, and administration in a way that she had seen at Mr. Brown's school. As she prepared to leave her office for the day, she was reviewing her daily emails, and came across one from Mr. Brown thanking her for spending some of her day with him—a thoughtful, simple email that supported his feelings that everyone mattered in his school environment.

Dr. Firemen was still for a very long time, thinking about how well she knew this quiet, outstanding principal. She had been a member of his student teaching class, had been in high school when he was hired as an associate principal, and finally worked alongside him as a head principal when she was in central office administration. Over the years, Mr. Brown's vision for school excellence and student achievement had been focused on engagement and building a sense of community and trust. She had never known him to waiver on those ideals. It finally dawned on her, his secret was being the Milkman.

Mr. Brown made sure each delivery of milk was timely, accepted, and personal. This was the way milkmen in times past delivered to individual homes.

- *Timely*: Interaction with each student daily. The conversation may have seemed insignificant to an outsider, but because it happened regularly, the students, faculty, and staff understood there was a real connection and warmth to the daily interaction with their principal.
- *Accepted*: This was the way business was conducted in the school. Everyone learned and worked together and cared about each other. Inquiring and helping others showed the leader's true self as being one who valued people at all levels. It was the accepted practice that the principal passed out milk at lunch to demonstrate his service to others.
- *Personal*: Mr. Brown knew each family at a personal level. He knew which students to ask about homework and which to ask about life in general. There was a feeling of mutual respect and love in the seemly light conversation. He made school personal to each and every person who walked through the doors.

As Dr. Firemen turned out her lights and closed her door for the evening, she vowed to return a note to Mr. Brown and thank him for teaching her the lesson of servantship that is the secret to his success as a principal.

QUESTIONS FOR REFLECTION

- What is Mr. Brown's secret to an effective and high achieving school?
- In the eyes of his school community, how do you feel Mr. Brown is received?
- When people commit to being servant leaders, what does that mean about the types of behaviors they exhibit within the school or organization they are leading?

FURTHER READING

Allen, G.P., Moore, W.M., Moser, L.R., Neill, K.K., Sambamoorthi, U., & Bell, H.S. (2016). The role of servant leadership and transformational leadership in academic pharmacy. *American Journal of Pharmacy Education*, 80, 113. Doi: 10. 5688/ajpe807113.

Whitlock, D. (2017). Types of effective leadership styles in schools. https://www.standardforsuccess.com

Closing Thoughts
9/11/2001

Jay Cloud

> *The most serious failure of leadership is the failure to foresee.*—Robert K. Greenleaf

We had moved into a new school in August. It was a beautiful building with big shiny halls allowing students to move from class to class without going outdoors. My room was not a 12' x 60' trailer; it was as big as a basketball court. We all felt we had been rewarded for our time of cramped quarters and trailer bathrooms. We were living the dream of every teacher.

One day, a calm, beautiful Tuesday morning as I remember it, I had arrived early to start putting a football practice agenda together. And as always, our principal, Mr. G, was walking the halls checking on the facilities, and saying hello to teachers. It was a new school, but it still had a punch list, so he constantly checked what was finished and what needed to be fixed while talking to staff. Students were starting to arrive, and Principal G was high-fiving and calling students by name as he went through the hallway.

About 8:50 a.m. that morning, my cell phone buzzed. I ignored it because I had kids in the room. After the third time, I looked and saw it was my wife, and it was urgent (the number displayed was our code). I stepped to the back of the room to answer. Amy, my wife, preceded to tell me something about an airplane, New York, buildings, and crashing. She was a wreck. As I was trying to understand what she was saying, I heard Mr. G come over the intercom requesting teachers to check their emails immediately. He was his usual, calm self, but I had to wonder if his email and what my wife was trying to describe over the phone were related.

I opened the email, and it read something like this: "Staff, there has been some type of plane crash at the World Trade Center in New York. They do not know what is happening, but I ask you to not turn on your television or bring it up on your computer. To help protect our customers (our name for students), we will not discuss anything about this. Please control your own emotions and continue the day as usual. I will give you a staff update in an hour through email."

What was this? Why can't we turn on our TV? What is so bad that my wife cannot tell me about it, and how should I continue my day as usual? That morning, the thoughts that raced through my head made it nearly impossible to concentrate on school activities, but I did my best to go about as expected. Am I missing a teachable moment for my kids? Why was Mr. G so adamant that we do not say anything to the students?

Through text messages from husbands and wives, the reality of the situation penetrated the school staff. Our school was only a few miles from the Southeast FAA control command, and Mr. G's former elementary school was just around the corner. The control command was the communication hub for all southeast airplanes. It was swarmed with national guard and security to help ward off any potential attacks crippling the airline communication system. Principal G sent out an updated email as promised, and it read something like this:

"Staff, I am so proud of how you are protecting our customers' innocence. I have suggested the school district evacuate ABC elementary due to its proximity to the FAA center. If they take my suggestion, they will start busing those students here in the next hour. Again, thank you for containing your emotions and opinions and protecting our customers. Do not discuss this with any student and treat today as a typical school day. Check back in 30 minutes for updates."

Again, Mr. G was so calm and relaxed. He walked through the hallway after sending that email just like he always did. He was chatting with students and telling them to get to class just as he always did.

I thought to myself, "How is he doing all this and still going about his routine?" I caught a glimpse of the band teacher across the hall; we both looked at each other with a puzzled look. Was that the same guy who just sent out an email a few minutes before, or were these emails coming from somewhere else? He was acting normal; his day had not changed even though something enormously big was happening outside the school's walls.

As the kids filed into their classes before the bell rang, I saw Mr. G headed my way. It was my planning period, and I hoped to find out what was going on, but he had other plans. He approached and said, "Mr. Cloud, they are bringing over the students from the elementary school, and we are going to use your classroom to host them. They think they are coming on a field trip to see the elective choices the middle school offers, so you and the other elective teachers will be working with their principal to assign teachers to teachers." He went on with some of the particulars, and soon the students started coming through the rear doors of our campus.

We were too busy to think about anything else but getting our students connected with their parents for the next few hours. By now, the news had spread in the community that we had students from both schools, and parents were starting to come and check out their children. I made several trips up to our dismissal line, escorting students to the front. Each time I could hear Mr. G addressing parents by name and telling our student helpers who their child was. He would make small talk and shake a hand or two, but he asked that they not discuss the events being reported on the news in the school.

By noon, all the students were out of the building and with their parents/guardians. Mr. G got on the intercom and asked all staff to report to our usual meeting place, the band room. He started with nothing but praise for how we had handled the evacuation of an elementary school and the early dismissal of both schools from our campus. A total of about 1,600 students had been fed, loved, sheltered, and released in just under four hours.

Mr. G went on to explain that it was not our job to break this type of news to the students. Instead, it was the parents who should discuss this tragic event with them in the home environment. We should not be seen as biased or judgmental when it comes to these matters, and more importantly, it was the parents' decision on how little or how much their child should know. Our job was to put their mental health needs as a priority. The school would be needed in the future to help the students deal with these events, but today was not the day.

"On another note, I was concerned for you all as well," Mr. G explained. "How would you describe some of the things that went on this morning to a middle schooler? How would you handle having multiple students asking questions or getting emotionally upset by watching the news?"

I saw Mr. G get red-faced with that statement, and some tears were beginning to flow. I now knew the rationale behind his decisions of the day. He was right. How would I explain to someone else's child why people were jumping to their death? What we had done for our entire school community started to sink in. Mr. G started walking around the room, shaking our hands, or giving out hugs to show his appreciation for what we had accomplished on this not-so-normal day. We all left that room emotional but proud of what we did and the leadership we witnessed. Once again, this was who Mr. G was. His servant leadership was undeniable.

I realize this example may seem to fall more into a good leader than servant leadership. But Mr. G's servant leadership did not just start that day. It might have been his defining moment, but it started years earlier when we were in the older building and going through situations at that school. We learned to trust each other. He trusted us to do the best we could with our customers, and we trusted he had the best interest of all of us. We knew that he knew the reality of the situation and focused on the main thing. Through these experiences, we would do anything he asked without question; we trusted him.

Mr. G was always listening. You could approach him about anything at any time. He might ponder the idea for a few days before bringing it to the group, but he was on board if it was suitable for the school. His wheelhouse was not dictatorial leadership; it was collaborative leadership. During faculty meetings, he gave us time to discuss situations, and he often implemented our solutions.

And on September 11, 2001, Mr. G showed empathy for the community, the students, and the teachers when he asked us not to expose our customers to the day's events. While my curiosity about the events was killing me, I followed his instructions. It was not until he explained his reasoning in the band room that I understood. What would I have told a 7th grade student when they saw buildings collapsing and the amount of death associated with that day? Would I have been able to perform my teaching responsibilities after watching the television? Not exposing the students to the traumatic footage on the television was one of the best leadership decisions I have been associated with in my career.

As best as he could, Mr. G offered us healing later that afternoon before he dismissed us. While we had not been glued in front of the television like most others, we knew enough to know that our lives would be different the next time we came back to that building. Bringing us together allowed us to process what we had done for our students and leave knowing we did a good thing. We had protected our students' innocence as long as possible. When we noticed Mr. G was going about his usual routine, it encouraged us to do the same.

And earlier, over the years, Mr. G's self-awareness of what we thought about what he was asking us to do was evident, so he led by example. If he asked us to do it, he must also do it. He did not have to persuade us or give us reasons, because he had laid the groundwork for years. We had been in the trenches with him before, and we knew to trust him through those smaller examples. He had always given reasons and rationale for critical decisions, so he had our trust and compliance when time was of the essence.

Mr. G was a staple of the school community for over eight years, so he knew most of the parents of both schools. When he stood out front and greeted parents and identified their children, he proved that he had built relationships based on trust and integrity. The parents seemed relieved when they noticed him standing there to greet them because they knew he oversaw the protection of their greatest asset. They were weeping as they came up the sidewalk to pick up their children—very emotional, but they knew we had cared for their child.

Afterword

Byron Darnall

Building a caring educational community like the one just described is very rare because teachers and administrators are so transient. Mr. G had built this trusted community of students, parents, and teachers not by just doing a few things now and then. He built this authentic culture because of who he was and his ability to embed leadership qualities into his daily walk. Peter Drucker shared the following advice with Jim Collins: "You seem to focus a lot on the question, 'How can I be successful?' That is the wrong question. The right question is 'How can I be useful?'"

Every leader should aspire to answer this very question. Leadership is not a position; it is an attitude, a disposition. The leaders presented in the previous pages demonstrate this clearly. Seth Godin refers to one's talents as art. School leaders persist in the art of caring and creating spaces that invite others to be a part of something larger than them themselves. This is not something we have to do, but something we get to do for others.

In seeking to become a servant leader, the hardest part may be learning that we are not owed gratitude. While gratitude often follows it should not be the primary motivator. Fulfillment lies in the serving of others through actions. America's schools are full of courageous, generous leaders that strive each day to be better knowing that perfect does not exist, but it is better than mediocrity.

References

Allen, G.P., Moore, W.M., Moser, L.R., Neill, K.K., Sambamoorthi, U., & Bell, H.S. (2016). The role of servant leadership and transformational leadership in academic pharmacy. *American Journal of Pharmacy Education*, 80 113. Doi: 10.5688/ajpe807113.

Batterson, M. (2016). *In a pit with a lion on a snowy day: How to survive and thrive when opportunity roars.* Colorado Springs: Multnomah.

Block, P. (1987). *Stewardship and the empowered manager.* Wiley.

Brooks, D. (2020). *The second mountain.* New York: Random House.

Bridwell-Mitchell, E.N. & Lant, T. (2013). Be careful what you wish for: The effects of issue interpretation on social choices in professional networks. https://doi.org/10.1287/orsc.2013.0840

Brown, Brené. (2018). *Dare to lead: Brave work, tough conversations, whole heart.* New York: Random House.

Bunting, B. (December 17, 2021). Climate Adaptation Center. https://www.theclimateadaptationcenter.org

Burgess, S. & Houf, B. (2017). *Lead like a pirate: Make school amazing for your students and staff.* Dave Burgess Consulting, Inc.

Burkhauser, S., Gates, S., Hamilton, L., & Igemoto, G. (2012). *Challenges and opportunities facing principals in the first year at a school.* Rand Corporation Research.

Carnegie, D. (1936). *How to win friends and influence people.* Simon and Schuster.

Center for Teaching and Learning. (2019). *The Western guide to mentoring graduate students across cultures.* London, Ontario, Canada. http://www.uwo.ca/tsc/purpleguides.html

Covey, S. (1994). *First things first.* Simon and Schuster.

Covey, S. (2014). *The leader in me: How schools around the world are inspiring greatness, one child at a time.* Simon and Schuster.

Doshi, P. (2020). The Power of shared decision-making through servant-leadership. https://www.scrum.org/resources/blog

Elliott, T., & Rossio, T. (2006). *Pirates of the Caribbean: At world's end.* Screenplay. Green Revision.

Focht, A., & Ponton, M. (2015). Identifying primary characteristics of servant leadership: Delphi Study. *International Journal of Leadership Studies*, 9(1): 44–61.

Goleman, D. (2005). *Emotional intelligence: Why it can matter more than IQ*. New York: Random House.

Greenleaf, R. (1977). *Servant leadership: A journey into the nature of legitimate power and greatness*. Paulist Press, New York.

Greenleaf, R. (2002). *Servant leadership, 25th anniversary edition*. Paulist Press.

Greenleaf, R. (2003). *The servant-leader within*. Paulist Press.

Greenleaf, R. K. (1998). *The power of servant-leadership: Essays*. Berrett-Koehler Publishers.

Greenleaf, R.K. (1970). *The Servant as Leader*. http://www.ediguys.net/Robert_K_Greenleaf_The_Servant_as_Leader.pdf

Grisson, J., Egalite, A., Lindsay, C. (2019). How principals affect students and schools: A systematic synthesis of two decades of research. Wallace Foundation. https://www.wallacefoundation.org/knowledge-center

Kafele, B. (2019). *The principal 50: Critical leadership questions for inspiring schoolwide excellence*. Association for School Curriculum and Development.

Kafele, B. (2020). *The assistant principal 50: Critical questions for meaningful leadership and professional growth*. ASIN: B088C1WBFM.

Lynch, M. (2019). *How servant leadership can transform your school district from the inside out*. The Edvocate Newsletter. https://www.theedadvocate.org

McElrath, K. (2020). Schooling during the COVID 19 pandemic. https://www.census.gov/library/stories.html

Meador, D. (2019). *Role of principal in schools*. https://www.thoughtco.com/role-of-principal-in-schools-3194583#:~:text=1%20Student%20Discipline%20Chief.%20A%20large%20part%20of,Public%20Relations%20Point%20Person.%20...%207%20Delegater.%20

National Policy Board for Educational Administration. (2015). Professional Standards for Education Leaders. Reston, VA. https://www.npbea.org/wp-content/uploads/2017/04/Professional-Standards-for-Educational-Leaders_2015.pdf

Parris, D.L. & Peachey, J.W. (2013). A Systematic Literature Review of Servant Leadership Theory in Organizational Contexts. Journal of Business Ethics, 113 (3): 377–393. https://doi.org/https://www.jstor.org/stable/23433856

Parker, W. (2016). *The 8 hats of a school leader: Principal matters*. https://williamdparker.com/2016/06/14/mpm-026

Roosevelt, T. Quote: Nobody cares how much you know, until . . . brainyquote.com

Sinek, S. (2011). *Start with why: How great leaders inspire everyone to take action*. Portfolio Publishing.

Singleton, G., & Singleton. C. (2006). *Courageous conversations about race*. Simon and Schuster.

Slawinski, F. (2021). *The assessment of the Bain Inspirational Leadership Model in a Finnish media agency*. https://inside,arcad.fi/kultur-och-med

Snyder, K., & Giella, M. (2013). *Developing principals' problem-solving capacities*. Association Supervision of Curriculum and Development.

Spears, L. (2010). Character and servant leadership: Ten characteristics of effective, caring leadership. Journal of Virtues & Leadership, 1(1). https://doi.org/https://ww.regent.edu/journal/journal-of-virtues-leadership/

character-and-servant-leadership-ten=characteristics-of-effective-caring-leaders/#references

Spears, L. & Reilly, M.J. (2018). "Make your life extraordinary: The teacher as servant-leader." *The International Journal of Servant-Leadership*, 12.

Spears, L. (2004). *Practicing servant leadership*. Wiley Publishing.

Spears, L. (2005, August). *The understanding and practice of servant-leadership*. https://www.regent.edu/wp-content/uploads/2020/12/spears_practice.pdf

Stewart, J.G. (2017). The importance of servant leadership in schools. *International Journal of Business Management and Commerce*, 2(5).

Stone, A. G., Russell, R. F., Patterson, K. (2003). Transformational versus servant leadership: A difference in leader focus. *Leadership and Organization Development Journal*, 25, 349–361.

Theophille, L. TED Talk (2020). How to lead from the heart. Chief Technology Transformation Office at Novartis. +Liz+Theophille&view=detail&mid=BAE9C 873F0DC3680CFCABAE9C873F0DC3680CFCA&FORM=VIRE&safeSearch=s trict&adlt=strict

Wall, P. (2016). One principal, two schools. The Atlantic. https://www.theatlantic.com/education/archive/2016/08

Wallace, R. (2008). *Principal to principal: Conversations in servant leadership and school transformation*. Rowman & Littlefield.

Wallace, R. (2009). *The servant leader and high school change*. Rowman & Littlefield.

Wallace, R. (2009). *Breaking away from the corporate model*. Rowman & Littlefield.

Wallace, R. (2012). *Servant leadership: Leaving a legacy*. Rowman & Littlefield.

Whitaker, T. (2003). *What great principals do differently: Fifteen things that matter most*. Larchment, NY: Eye on Education.

Whitlock, D. (2017). *Types of effective leadership styles in schools*. https://www.standardforsuccess.com

Wiseman, L., Allen, L., & Foster, E. (2013). *The multiplier effect: Tapping the genius inside our schools*. Corwin.

Zhong, L., Qian, Z., & Wang, D. (2020). How does the servant supervisor influence the employability of postgraduates? Exploring the mechanisms of self-efficacy and academic engagement. *Front. Bus. Res. China* 14 (11). https://doi.org/10.1186/s11782-020-00079-1

About the Editor and Contributors

Dr. Joseph "Rocky" Wallace is Associate Professor of Education at Campbellsville University. He came to CU in the fall of 2018 from Asbury University, where he had served for 7 1/2 years as the coordinator of the principal licensure/Ed.S. degree program. Previous to Asbury, he taught in Morehead State's graduate education leadership program (full-time instructor, beginning as an adjunct). Rocky is a former principal of a Kentucky and U.S. Blue Ribbon School (Catlettsburg Elementary), and District PTA Principal of the Year (Fallsburg Elementary/Middle), served in the Highly Skilled Educator program at the Kentucky Department of Education (KDE) as a leadership consultant to new principals, and as director of instructional support and adult education at the Kentucky Education Development Cooperative in Ashland, Kentucky.

Rocky's research area is servant leadership and organizational health, and he consults with schools and presents on the topic regularly at education and leadership conferences. He has written, co-authored, and co-edited 10 books with education publisher Rowman & Littlefield in the domains of school improvement and servant leadership. He has a Doctorate in Strategic Leadership from Regent University.

Eve Proffitt is currently the Project Specialist, Office of Educator Licensure and Effectiveness, Kentucky Department of Education. She has worked in education for 48 years. Eve has been the director of P20 Lab and clinical professor of educational leadership at the University of Kentucky, dean of education and professor of graduate education at Georgetown College, special education director and director of data with the Kentucky School Boards Association, and associate superintendent of special pupil service, federal projects coordinator, principal, elementary and special education teacher with the Fayette County School district. She served as International President of Phi Delta Kappa.

Eve received her BA and MA from Eastern Kentucky University and her Ed.S. and Ed.D. from the University of Kentucky. She is a national curriculum auditor as well as curriculum trainer with CMSi and Phi Delta Kappa. She has conducted and/or participated in over 75 curriculum audits since 1978.

Stephanie Sullivan has been an educator for over 30 years, formerly serving in the K–12 setting as a teacher, counselor, and administrator. As principal, she led her school to achieve National Blue Ribbon School status, and she was named 2009 Administrator of the Year by the National Association of Elementary School Principals. Since 2017, she has served as an instructor/assistant professor at Murray State University, where she now serves as the Coordinator of the Education Administration program.

Stephanie collaborates with districts in the region and the Kentucky Department of Education (KDE) to build leadership capacity through the Institute for School Leadership Development and the Kentucky LEADS Academy. Her research focuses on the K–12 environment and school leadership. In collaboration with the University Principal Preparation Initiative (UPPI) and KDE, she has authored two book chapters and co-edited the book, *School Improvement: Let the PSEL Standards Work for You.*

* * *

Carrie Ballinger is currently the Superintendent of Rockcastle County Schools and the former Director of Student Services for the Rockcastle County School District. In addition, Mrs. Ballinger previously served as the elementary principal of Kingston Elementary in Madison County, Kentucky, and the Elementary Director of Model Laboratory School on the campus of Eastern Kentucky University. She received both a Bachelor's and Master's degree in Elementary Education from Eastern Kentucky University.

Carrie is a National Board Certified Teacher and holds an Ed.S. degree in Educational Leadership from Asbury University. Mrs. Ballinger served as an elementary teacher for 10 years where she specialized in reading instruction. During this time, she also served as a member of the Rockcastle County Board of Education for over 6 years. Mrs. Ballinger's passion for education stems from lessons learned from her grandfather, Mr. Thomas Land, whose formal education ended in the 8th grade. She keeps her grandfather's lunch pail on a shelf in her office as a reminder to never lose sight of how important the value of education is.

Myram Brady came to Lawrence County High School (LCHS) in the fall of 2016 from Fallsburg Elementary, where she had served for 12 years as a teacher. She started as the Freshman Coordinator at LCHS and is now an assistant principal at the school. She served in the areas of teaching special education and then regular education until moving into an administration role.

Myram is a graduate of Morehead State University, where she earned a Bachelor's degree in Teaching and a Master's in Special Education from 2000–2005. She decided to return to school to earn a second Master's degree, in School Administration, from Asbury University in 2015, and continued on to earn her Ed.S. degree from Asbury.

Myram has served as an intermediate grades team lead as well as team lead for elementary math. She serves as a coach for Positive Behavior Interventions and Supports (PBIS) and district safe crisis manager trainer. She also works as a coach for Building Assets Reducing Risk (BARR) in her high school. She currently serves on several committees for building support for high school students with transition.

Ann Burns is an Associate Professor in Educational Leadership at Eastern Kentucky University (EKU). She serves in the Department of Teaching, Learning, and Educational Leadership in the College of Education and Applied Human Sciences.

Prior to joining EKU, Ann worked for 28 years in public P–12 schools in the state of Kentucky. She is a former classroom teacher, building principal, district level administrator, and Kentucky Department of Education director. She has also served as the Director of Instructional Support at the Kentucky Education Development Corporation. Her work includes a focus on school improvement, developing systems for continuous improvement, and improving school culture.

Carol Christian is currently the Director of the Craft Academy for Excellence in Science and Mathematics at Morehead State University, a program for high achieving high school juniors and seniors pursuing a STEM career. She has served as a professor in Morehead's doctoral program in Educational Leadership, coordinating the program in its initial beginnings.

Carol served in the Highly Skilled Educator program and as a school improvement specialist with the Kentucky Department of Education, and is a National Institute for School Leaders (NISL) trainer (patterned after the U.S. Army War College leadership training). Her body of research has been in the area of social justice. She has co-authored five books for school administrators.

Jerry "Jay" Cloud graduated from Murray State University in 1995 with a Bachelor's degree in Middle School Education. Since then, he has earned a Master's degree in Curriculum and Instruction from the University of

Phoenix and a Master's degree in Career and Technical Education from Eastern Kentucky University. He has earned a Specialist degree in Supervisor of Instruction, K–12 Principal, along with his Area Technical School Administrator Endorsement from Eastern Kentucky University.

Jay started his teaching career in Lone Oak Middle School teaching history in a long-term substitute position. He then moved to Warren County, Tennessee, to teach math and science. He left there and moved to McDonough, Georgia, to work as a middle school science teacher and later, the technology lab teacher. While working at The Kentucky School for the Deaf, he turned his focus to career and technical education and working with local businesses to give students skills to help them find employment. Jay currently works at W.E.B. DuBois Academy for Jefferson County Public Schools as the Verizon Innovation Learning Lab mentor instructor. His current doctoral research at Morehead State University explores how schools can successfully imbed the employability skills in their everyday curriculum.

Byron Darnall joined the Kentucky Department of Education's (KDE) Office of Educator Licensure and Effectiveness (OELE) as Associate Commissioner in June 2021. A native of Meade County, he has served in various education roles in Kentucky and a stint in the Iowa Department of Education.

Byron earned a Bachelor's degree in English from David Lipscomb University, and later a Master's degree in Education from the University of Kentucky. He also earned his Rank 1 certification from Western Kentucky University and a Doctorate in Education Leadership from Seton Hall University. Prior to joining KDE, Byron served as a teacher, assistant principal, and principal in several Kentucky public schools. From 2012 to 2014 he served as a bureau chief at the Iowa Department of Education.

Jason Detre came to Campbellsville University in 2017, serving as adjunct professor in the School of Education. He is also an adjunct with the University of the Cumberlands. He has served two years as the principal at New Haven School (P–8) in Larue County, and seven years as principal at LaRue County Middle School (6–8)—named a School of Distinction during his tenure.

Jason is currently serving Iroquois High School in Jefferson County as an assistant principal over curriculum, instruction, and educational coaching. He has also served on the board of directors for the Kentucky Association of School Administrators (KASA), serving in leadership roles from a regional representative to KASA president in the 2019–2020 school year. He has also served on numerous educational advisory boards within Kentucky. His research area is educational coaching and the impacts of coaching on instructional practices within the classroom.

Josh Gupton has been employed with the Green County School District since 2007. He served grades K–5 as a music educator and school counselor for ten years. He currently serves as the assistant principal of Green County Intermediate School, a position he has held since 2018. Josh is also a Kentucky certified firefighter and emergency medical technician. He has previously served as a vocational instructor for grades 9–12 in the areas of emergency services. As a Kentucky certified fire and emergency medical supervisor (EMS) instructor, he continues to serve his community through the training of all ages of firefighters and medical professionals in his home county and beyond.

Josh holds a Bachelor's degree in Music Education, Masters of Arts in Education, Masters of Arts in School Counseling, and a Masters of Arts in Education Administration. He is continuing doctoral study in Educational Leadership at Western Kentucky University.

Laura Beth Hayes is currently assistant principal at Creekside Elementary in Hardin County, Kentucky. She is a third-generation educator who received her Bachelor's degree in Elementary Education from Campbellsville University (CU) in 2003. Shortly after, she received her Master's degree from CU in 2006. In 2008 she earned her Rank I through the Education Professional Standards Board CEO Option. In 2012, she earned her National Board Certification Teacher (NBCT) in Early Childhood. After teaching elementary school for 18 years, Laura Beth earned her graduate school administration degree from CU during the pandemic and graduated in 2021.

Laura Beth received the WHAS-11 ExCEL Award in 2015, as well as the Campbellsville Excellence in Teaching Award in 2006. She has been a guest speaker at CU for the Excellence in Teaching ceremony and the 2021 commencement exercises. She has also presented at numerous conferences and served as a guest speaker in different undergraduate and graduate classes. Currently, she is pursuing her Ed.D. in Educational Leadership and Diversity at Western Kentucky University.

Tabetha Housekeeper is currently the Director of Student Services for Scott County Schools and a former principal of Lemons Mill Elementary School in Georgetown, Kentucky. She is a first-generation college graduate. She received a Bachelor's degree in Elementary Education from Georgetown College, along with a Master's degree in Learning and Behavior Disorders. After two years of teaching special education and ten years of teaching in elementary, Tabetha completed her graduate school administrative degree from Asbury University.

Tabetha worked three years with the Next Generation Leadership Academy through the University of Kentucky to provide professional development and speak at state conferences in several states. She also led teacher leader groups through three years of learning and participation in a local grant related to Culturally Responsive Instructional Observation Protocols (CRIOP). In 2016, Tabetha became the Project Lead The Way Teacher of the Year after her work with local engineers and the Toyota Manufacturing company. She is currently pursuing a Ph.D. in Leadership at the University of Cumberlands.

Mike Hylen currently serves as the Coordinator of Doctoral Studies and Graduate School Faculty at Southern Wesleyan University (SWU). Before joining the SWU faculty, he served as a professor in the graduate schools at Louisiana State University and Asbury University in Kentucky. In addition, Mike served in a number of leadership roles at each institution, including department chair and interim dean. He has published research on social-emotional learning, servant leadership, and teacher preparation. He recently had a new book released titled, *Cultivating Emotional Intelligence* (Rowman & Littlefield).

Prior to joining the higher education ranks, Mike enjoyed a 25-year career as a public and private school educator. His experiences on the K–12 level included serving in urban, rural, and suburban settings. His most extensive work was as an alternative high school principal for students who struggled not only academically, but also emotionally and behaviorally. He earned his Ph.D. from the University of Missouri-St. Louis with a specific emphasis on at-risk students and social-emotional learning.

Mike Kessinger currently serves as Associate Professor of Educational Leadership at Morehead State University. Joining Morehead in 2014, he serves as program lead for both the Education Leadership and Doctor of Education programs. He has also served as adjunct instructor at Prestonsburg Community College, Southwest West Virginia Community College in Williamson, and the University of Kentucky—teaching in the areas of mathematics, computer science, educational research, school law, psychology, and educational leadership.

Prior to coming to Morehead, Michael worked in the Martin County School System in Inez, Kentucky. There, he was a secondary mathematics and computer science teacher, high school assistant principal, gifted education coordinator, finance director, and assistant superintendent. He also held several coaching positions including baseball, cross county, and tennis. Michael received his Ed.S. from the University of Kentucky, Ed. S. and Masters of Education from Morehead State University, and Bachelor of Science from the University of Wisconsin-Eau Claire with a teaching emphasis in mathematics and computer science.

Kelly Odell is currently the principal of Mercer County Intermediate School in Harrodsburg, Kentucky, where she has served for two years. She began her career in Missouri, teaching 2nd grade for a year and a half. Kelly then taught in Tennessee, where she served in 1st, 2nd, and 4th grade classes. She taught 2nd grade for one year and 5th grade for five years at Woodlawn Elementary School in Danville, Kentucky, before making the move to Mercer County as an administrator.

Kelly holds her Bachelor's degree in Elementary Education from Harding University in Searcy, Arkansas. Her first Master's degree was in Instructional Leadership from Eastern Kentucky University, and her second Master's degree in School Leadership was from Campbellsville University. She is fully trained in Kagan Cooperative Learning and the Orton-Gillingham approach and is Google certified Level 1. She served as lead teacher for 12 years of her teaching career and served on Boyle County's district leadership team. She was chosen as a member of the Inquiry Based Learning Committee, a pilot program for Boyle County's school district. Currently, Kelly is leading Mercer County Intermediate School to becoming a Leader in Me school.

J.P. Rader has served as a teacher, coach, and administrator for thirty years at overseas international schools in Korea and Singapore, as well as ten years in higher education in the U.S. He has recently completed his third year as the Head of School at International Community School (Singapore), which is part of the Network of International Christian Schools (NICS). J.P. previously served as the secondary principal at Gyeonggi Suwon International School in Korea. Earlier in his career he also served as a teacher, coach, and administrator at Taejon Christian International School and Seoul Foreign School for 23 years.

Before returning overseas, J.P. spent seven years at Asbury University as Associate Professor of Secondary Education, as well as serving as the head women's volleyball coach. During this period he worked with the Race to the Top Grant for school improvement in Eastern Kentucky and served on multiple PETLL (Perpetuating Excellence in Teaching, Leadership and Learning) school improvement teams. His volleyball teams at Asbury qualified for two national tournaments and won over 200 matches. He earned his Ed.D. from Morehead State University.

William C. Sims is currently the principal of Southern Pulaski Middle School (SPMS) (the tenth largest middle school in Kentucky). He is also an adjunct professor at the University of the Cumberlands, teaching graduate courses in educational administration. Prior to being the head principal, he was an assistant principal at SPMS for two years. William was an English language arts (ELA) middle grades teacher in the Lincoln and Pulaski school districts for over 20 years. He graduated from Berea College in 1993, and holds graduate degrees from Eastern Kentucky University and Western Kentucky University. He earned his Doctorate in Educational Leadership from the University of the Cumberlands.

Professionally, William's areas of interest are in educational leadership, teacher development, school climate and culture, and teacher recruitment. He was recently elected to the Kentucky Association of School Administrators (KASA) Executive Board of Directors as the middle grades administrator representative. His doctoral research was in the field of vocabulary and assessments, and he is currently working on a series of coaching books for middle school ELA teachers on vocabulary instructional strategies and techniques.

Larry Spears is an editor and/or contributing author to 38 books on servant leadership, including *Conversations on Servant-Leadership* (2015), and the best-selling *Insights on Leadership* (1998). He is the editor and curator of all five books of writings by Robert K. Greenleaf. Since 2008, Larry has served as Servant-Leadership Scholar for Gonzaga University's School for Leadership Studies (Spokane), where he teaches graduate courses in servant leadership and listening, and serves as Senior Advisory Editor for The International Journal of Servant-Leadership.

Larry is also president of The Spears Center for Servant-Leadership, Indianapolis. From 1990 to 2007, he served as president and CEO and as senior fellow and president emeritus of The Robert K. Greenleaf Center. A 2004 interview with him on NBC Dateline was seen by ten million viewers.

Franklin Thomas is currently Assistant Graduate Chair and Assistant Professor of Education at Campbellsville University (CU) in Kentucky, where he primarily teaches courses for aspiring school principals and district administrators. In the CU School of Education, he chairs the Council for the Accreditation of Educator Preparation (CAEP) Standard 1 committee. He authored a chapter, "Ethical and Professional Norms" in the book, *School Improvement: Let the Professional Standards for Educational Leaders Work for You*. His current research projects include "Improving Mentoring and Other Support of Alternatively Certified School Principals in Kentucky," and "Grow Your Own Programs: An Opportunity for Universities and School Districts to Collaborate and Reshape Principal Preparation."

Franklin holds a Bachelor's degree in Mathematics with distinction and departmental honors, and a Master's degree in Secondary Education from the University of Kentucky. He also holds a Rank I in Educational Administration and an Ed.D. in Educational Leadership and Policy Studies from Eastern Kentucky University. He began in public P–12 education in 1989 as a substitute teacher and retired 30 years later as a director of human resources/director of pupil personnel and overseer of a district Save-the-Children Program. In between, Franklin was a high school teacher, department chair, and school council member, Highly Skilled Educator at the Kentucky Department of Education (team leader), high school assistant principal, middle school principal, curriculum coordinator, instructional supervisor, and district assessment coordinator.

Lewis Willian has served as an Assistant Professor in the School of Education at Asbury University for the past five years. Currently, he serves as Program Director for Educational Leadership, providing leadership for the post-master's graduate programs at the university. He served as a teacher, administrator, and district leader in the Clark County School System throughout his 30-year P–12 career.

Lewis twice worked on loan to the Kentucky Department of Education as a school change agent, once as a Highly Skilled Educator and later as an Education Recovery Leader, serving in support of student success in various districts throughout the state. His research interests include increasing student ownership of their learning and developing a positive school culture. Previously, he co-authored *Student Ownership: Five Strands to Success for All Students* with education publisher Rowman & Littlefield. He has an Ed.D. from Morehead State University.

Whitney Shannon Wilson has been the principal of Simons Middle School in Flemingsburg, Kentucky, since 2015. Prior, she served as an assistant principal and library media specialist. She attended Morehead State University, where she received a Bachelor's degree in Secondary Education and a Master's degree in School Leadership and Administration. She also attended Western Kentucky University where she received a Master's degree in Library Science, and Eastern Kentucky University where she earned certification as Superintendent of Schools.

Currently, Whitney is enrolled in the doctorate program at Morehead State University for P–12 Administration, with an anticipated graduation in 2023. Her doctoral study includes researching how leadership impacts job satisfaction and culture in schools. School improvement, collaboration, and community are an important part of her life as she continues to serve the community in which she grew up.

Lu Settles Young is clinical Associate Professor at the University of Kentucky (UK) in the Department of Educational Leadership Studies, and Executive Director of the UK Center for Next Generation Leadership. She is the program faculty chair for the UK principal preparation program, and she also teaches in the superintendent certification program.

Before coming to UK, Lu served as Chief Academic Officer of Fayette County Public Schools in Lexington, Kentucky, and before that, Superintendent of Jessamine County Schools for nine years. She earned principal and superintendent certifications from the University of Kentucky and holds a Doctorate in Education Leadership from Northern Kentucky University.

Lu was appointed to the Kentucky Board of Education by Governor Andy Beshear in December 2019 and became board chair in April 2020. She is actively involved with the Kentucky Association of School Superintendents and serves on the Kentucky Commonwealth Education Continuum and the Education Commission of the States. She was selected as Kentucky's Superintendent of the Year in 2012.

Rosemarie Young is Assistant Professor and Chair of the Ed.S. and MAEd programs at Bellarmine University in Louisville, Kentucky. She has been associated with Bellarmine University since 2013. She worked in the Jefferson County Public School district for 38 years, 28 years as an elementary school principal. While with the JCPS, she was named the Elementary School Principal of the Year. Rosie was elected president-elect of the National Association of Elementary School Principals in 2003, and served as national president of NAESP during the 2004–2005 school year (the only national president from Kentucky). Serving as the executive director of the Kentucky Association of Elementary School Principals, she works to support elementary and middle school leaders in Kentucky.

Rosie was named Kentucky's National Distinguished Principal for 2012. As an NDP, she traveled to Washington, DC, and was recognized in a special ceremony sponsored by the National Association of Elementary School Principals. She served on the national committee that developed the National Educational Leadership Preparation (NELP) standards. She earned her BA from Bellarmine University, her M.Ed from the University of Louisville, and her Ed.D. from Spalding University. Rosie holds certifications in elementary education, special education, school guidance counselor, principalship, exceptional child education supervisor, and superintendency. Currently, she teaches in the Educational Specialist (Ed.S.) program that prepares candidates for school leadership positions.

www.ingramcontent.com/pod-product-compliance
Lightning Source LLC
Chambersburg PA
CBHW030141240426
43672CB00005B/224